**THE HIGH SCHOOL
MATHEMATICS LIBRARY**

THE HIGH SCHOOL

MATHEMATICS LIBRARY

William L. Schaaf

Professor Emeritus
Brooklyn College
The City University of New York
Brooklyn, New York

NATIONAL COUNCIL OF TEACHERS OF MATHEMATICS

1906 Association Drive, Reston, Virginia 22091

Copyright © 1960. 1963, 1967, 1970, 1973, 1976, 1982, 1987, by
THE NATIONAL COUNCIL OF
TEACHERS OF MATHEMATICS, INC.
All Rights Reserved
Eighth Edition
Printed in the United States of America

Library of Congress Cataloging in Publication Data:

Schaaf, William Leonard, 1898–
The high school mathematics library.
1. Mathematics—Bibliography. I. Title.
Z6651.S37 1987 [QA36] 016.51   87-1651
ISBN 0-87353-238-4

The publications of the National Council of Teachers of Mathematics present a variety
of viewpoints. The views expressed or implied in this publication,
unless otherwise noted, should not be interpreted as official positions of the Council.

Contents

Expository Mathematics 1
Foundations and Philosophy of Mathematics; Logic 10
History and Cultural Evolution of Mathematics 12
Biographies and Personalities.. 16
Science and Mathematics 19
Recreational Mathematics 22
Arithmetic; Numeration; Computation..................................... 30
Algebra; Calculus; Analysis 31
Geometry... 35
Topology; Networks; Polyhedrons 40
Theory of Numbers 43
Probability; Statistics... 44
Metric Measures... 47
Computer Science 48
   General Publications, 48
   Social Impact of Computers, 50
   Computers in the Classroom and the Home, 50
   Computer Recreations, 53
Professional Books for Teachers 54
   Mathematical Education; Trends; Curriculum; Administration, 54
   Psychology of Learning Mathematics, 57
   Problem-solving Techniques, 60
   Teaching Secondary School Mathematics, 61
   Activities; Projects; Enrichment; Contests; Visual Aids, 64
Dictionaries and Handbooks.. 67
Publications of the NCTM 68
   Yearbooks, 68
   Classics in Mathematical Education, 69
   Enrichment and Recreation, 70
   Research, 71
   General Publications, 72
   Readings from NCTM Periodicals, 75
Publications of the Mathematical Association of America................. 75
Periodicals and Journals.. 76
Appendix: Directory of Current Publishers 79

Foreword

Mathematical education has passed through dramatic changes during the quarter century since the first edition of this booklet appeared in 1960. When by the early seventies the "new math" had come and gone, the pendulum understandably went from too much emphasis on abstractions, logic, and structure to serious concern for minimal competencies and mathematical literacy. As the eighties approached, the urgency for basics mellowed somewhat, and attention focused on problem-solving strategies and cognitive learning. Now we face the impact of the computer in the mathematics classroom.

Such changes clearly affect the selection of books for the high school mathematics library. This applies to supplementary material for students, books for parents and the general reader, and professional books for teachers, teacher educators, administrators, librarians, and authors.

This booklet is addressed primarily to high school students of all levels of ability and to their mathematics teachers. It should also be of interest to students and instructors of mathematics in two-year colleges. Finally, librarians of both public and school libraries should also find this catalog a useful guide.

This edition adds some two hundred titles of books published since 1980 and eliminates obsolete titles. Therefore, the entire list still numbers about a thousand books. Moreover, it preserves good balance, as follows:

Appreciation (exposition; philosophy; history) 30%
Motivation (mathematical recreations) 12%
Content (specific mathematical areas) 30%
Learning (computers; psychology; teaching) 28%

These figures do not include the list of publications of the National Council of Teachers of Mathematics and the New Mathematics Library list of the Mathematical Association of America.

As in previous editions, the practice of starring certain titles has been retained solely as guidance where library budgets are limited. These arbitrary designations carry no implications about the relative merit of any book.

Considering today's uncertainties in mathematics education as well as the renewed public interest in general education, the role of books and libraries assumes greater importance than ever. It would be unfortunate indeed if budgetary constraints or the attitude of a frustrated society were to preclude continued support and expansion of library facilities. The printed word has not been wholly replaced by electronic media.

W. L. S.

Boca Raton, Florida

In these days of conflict between ancient and modern studies, there must surely be something to be said for a study which did not begin with Pythagoras, and will not end with Einstein, but is the oldest and the youngest of all.

G. H. Hardy
A Mathematician's Apology

Note to the Reader

For references to less advanced materials, see the companion bibliography, *Mathematics Library—Elementary and Junior High School.*

Expository Mathematics

Adler, Irving, ed. *Readings in Mathematics: Book 2.* Ginn, 1972, 188 pp., paper.

Andree, Josephine, ed. *Chips from the Mathematical Log.* Mu Alpha Theta, 1966, 96 pp., paper.

———. *Lines from the O.U. Mathematics Letter.* 3 vols. Mu Alpha Theta, 1971, 106 pp., 42 pp., 102 pp., paper.

———. *More Chips from the Mathematical Log.* Mu Alpha Theta, 1970, 87 pp., paper.

Asimov, Isaac. *Asimov on Numbers.* Doubleday, 1977, 249 pp.
> Reprints of seventeen popular essays from the *Magazine of Fantasy and Science Fiction*, including discourses on zero, imaginary numbers, giant numbers, and various calendars.

Bakst, Aaron. *Mathematics: Its Magic and Mastery.* 3d ed. Van Nostrand, 1967, 842 pp.
> A comprehensive and readable exposition.

Beard, Col. R. S., *Patterns in Space.* Creative Pubs., 1973, 237 pp., softbound.
> A unique collection of designs and configurations.

Beck, Anatole, Michael Bleicher, and Donald Crowe. *Excursions into Mathematics.* Worth, 1969, 489 pp.
> Six independent essays on polyhedrons, perfect numbers, area, a variety of geometrics, mathematical games, and numeration systems.

☆ Bell, Eric T. *Mathematics: Queen and Servant of Science.* McGraw, 1951, 437 pp.
> A revision and amplification of *The Queen of the Sciences* and *The Handmaiden of the Sciences*, skillfully rewritten into one volume.

☆ Bergamini, David, and the editors of *Life. Mathematics.* Life Sciences Library. Silver, 1963, 200 pp.
> Distinctive pictorial material with accompanying text.

Berkeley, Edmund C. *A Guide to Mathematics for the Intelligent Non-Mathematician.* Simon, 1967, 352 pp.

Berlinghoff, William P. *Mathematics: The Art of Reason.* Heath, 1968, 260 pp.
> Concise and stimulating; for mature readers.

Boehm, George A. W., and the editors of *Fortune. The New World of Mathematics.* Dial, 1959, 128 pp., paper.
> Essays on the nature of modern mathematics and on contemporary applied mathematics.

Bosstick, Maurice, and John L. Cable. *Patterns in the Sand: An Exploration in Mathematics.* Glencoe, 1975, 384 pp.
>A general survey; two-year college level; stimulating discussion of sets, logic, number systems, probability, statistics, mathematical systems, and so on.

Bower, Julia Wells. *Mathematics—a Creative Art.* Holden, 1973, 315 pp.
>For the general college student and interested nonprofessional; stresses the imaginative nature of mathematics and its aesthetic appreciation.

Bradis, V. M., V. L. Minkovskii, and A. K. Kharcheva. *Lapses in Mathematical Reasoning.* Pergamon, 1963, 201 pp., paper.
>An interesting collection of over eighty specific examples of false reasoning and paradoxes in arithmetic, algebra, geometry, and trigonometry.

☆ Burkhardt, Hugh. *The Real World and Mathematics.* Birkhauser (Blackie & Son, Ltd.), 1981, 189 pp.

☆ Campbell, Douglas, and John Higgins. *Mathematics: People, Problems, Results, vols. 1, 2, and 3. Wadsworth International, 1984, 871 pp.*
>Extensive collection of readings *about* mathematics: how mathematics developed; philosophical and psychological implications.

Cook, Theodore Andrea. *The Curves of Life.* Dover, 1979, 479 pp., softbound.
>Republication of a classic long out of print; mathematical forms in Nature and in architecture.

Coughlin, Raymond, and David Zitarelli. *The Ascent of Mathematics.* McGraw, 1984, 609 pp.

☆ Courant, Richard, and Herbert Robbins. *What Is Mathematics? An Elementary Approach to Ideas and Methods.* Oxford, 1941, 521 pp.
>For mature readers; excellent discussion of the number system, geometric constructions, postulational systems, number theory, and topology.

☆ Dantzig, Tobias. *Number, the Language of Science.* 4th ed. Macmillan, 1967, 340 pp.
>Excellent exposition of the concept of number; difficult reading in spots.

Davis, Philip J., and William G. Chinn. *3.1416 and All That.* Simon, 1969, 184 pp.

Dorrie, Heinrich. *100 Great Problems of Elementary Mathematics.* Dover, 1965, 389 pp.

Dowdy, S. M. *Mathematics: Art and Science.* Wiley, 1971, 282 pp.
>A somewhat sophisticated exposition.

☆ Durbin, John R. *Mathematics, Its Spirit and Evolution.* Allyn, 1973, 321 pp.

Evans, Dorothy. *Mathematics: Friend or Foe?* Allen, 1977, 140 pp., cloth and paper.
>Very readable; for the junior high school level.

☆ Eves, Howard W. *In Mathematical Circles.* 2 vols. Prindle, 1969, 136 pp., 145 pp.
   A collection of 360 delightful anecdotes; will appeal to readers of every age.

———. *Mathematical Circles Adieu.* Prindle, 1977, 181 pp.
   Collection of anecdotes, similar to the author's previous collections.

☆ ———. *Mathematical Circles Revisited: A Second Collection of Mathematical Stories and Anecdotes.* Prindle, 1971, 186 pp.

☆ ———. *Mathematical Circles Squared.* Prindle, 1972, 186 pp.

Felix, Lucienne. *The Modern Aspects of Mathematics.* Basic, 1960, 194 pp.
   Sophisticated essays on the nature of contemporary mathematics together with implications for mathematical education.

Flagg, Graham. *Numbers: Their History and Meaning.* Schocken, 1983, 295 pp.

☆ Fox, Lynn H., et al., eds. *Women and the Mathematical Mystique.* Hopkins, 1980, 211 pp., softbound.
   Expanded version of the 1976 AAAS Symposium, "Women and Mathematics."

Freudenthal, Hans. *Mathematics Observed.* World, 1968, 256 pp.
   For the mature reader; fascinating discussions of such assorted topics as computers, nim, iterative processes, infinity, topology, mechanics, and world measurement.

☆ Fuchs, Walter R. *Mathematics for the Modern Mind.* Macmillan, 1967, 286 pp.
   Lucid and fascinating excursion through the sweep of modern mathematics, including basic concepts and foundations, logic, structure, sets, group theory, number theory, game theory, topology, and mathematical philosophy.

Gardner, Martin. *The Ambidextrous Universe: Mirror Asymmetry and Time-Reversed Worlds.* 2d ed. Scribner, 1979, 300 pp.
   A revised, updated edition of a well-known, fascinating exposition of asymmetry as applied to planets, plants, crystals, molecules, and so forth.

Ghyka, Matila. *The Geometry of Art and Life.* Dover, 1977, 176 pp., paper.
   Proportion in art and architecture with emphasis on the golden section, dynamic symmetry, and regular polyhedrons.

☆ Glenn, William H., and Donovan A. Johnson. *Exploring Mathematics on Your Own.* Dover, 1973, 303 pp., paper.
   Originally published in separate pamphlet form; junior/senior high school level.

☆ ———. *Invitation to Mathematics.* Dover, 1962, 373 pp., paper.
   Originally published as separate pamphlets; junior/senior high school level.

☆ Goodman, A. W. *The Pleasures of Math.* Collier, 1965, cloth; Macmillan, 1965, 224 pp., paper.
   A stimulating, witty introduction to challenging mathematical topics and recreations, including inequalities, mathematical induction, the four-color problem, magic squares, conic sections, and so on.

Graham, Malcolm. *Mathematics: A Liberal Arts Approach*. Harcourt, 1973, 278 pp.
: Appreciation of mathematics; methods of reasoning; role of mathematics in history.

Gross, Herbert I., and Frank L. Miller. *Mathematics: A Chronicle of Human Endeavor*. Holt, 1971, 367 pp.

Gudder, Stanley. *A Mathematical Journey*. McGraw, 1976, 434 pp.
: A stimulating resource book; emphasis both on understanding and appreciating such areas as the theory of numbers, graph theory, group theory, and computer science.

☆ Guillen, Michael. *Bridges to Infinity: The Human Side of Mathematics*. Houghton, 1983, 204 pp.
: Illuminating exposition.

Hadamard, Jacques. *The Psychology of Invention in the Mathematical Field*. Dover, 1954, 145 pp.

☆ Hall, Richard S. *About Mathematics*. Prentice, 1973, 270 pp.
: The nature of mathematics, for non-mathematics students; ideas are presented around the lives of great mathematicians.

Halmos, P. R. *Selecta: Expository Writing*. Edited by D. E. Sarason and Leonard Gillman. Springer, 1983, 304 pp.
: Stimulating; for mature students, teachers, and authors.

☆ Hardy, G. H. *A Mathematician's Apology*. Foreword by C. P. Snow. Cambridge, 1967, 153 pp.
: New edition of a justly renowned classic.

Herstein, I. N., and I. Kaplansky. *Matters Mathematical*. Harper, 1974, 246 pp.
: For nonmajors in mathematics; concerned with sets and functions, number theory, permutations, group theory, finite geometry, game theory, and infinite sets.

Hogben, Lancelot. *Mathematics for the Million*. 4th ed. Norton, 1968, 660 pp.
: A pioneer best-seller among popular books on mathematics; somewhat more demanding on the reader than its title suggests.

☆ Holt, M., and T. D. E. Marjoram. *Mathematics in a Changing World*. Heinemann, 1973, 293 pp.
: Essays for nonprofessionals, stressing applications of mathematics in contemporary society.

Holt, M., and A. J. McIntosh. *The Scope of Mathematics*. Oxford, 1966, 266 pp.
: A fresh look at mathematics for the nonspecialist; historical as well as mathematical; fairly mature reading.

Honsberger, Ross. *Ingenuity in Mathematics*. Singer, 1970, 204 pp.
: Brief, self-contained essays on significant topics of elementary mathematics; lively reading.

☆ ——. *Mathematical Gems*. MAA, 1973, 176 pp.
: Thirteen sophisticated essays dealing with a wide variety of topics, such as Hamiltonian circuits, the magic hexagon, lattice points, perfect numbers, Morley's theorem, combinatorics, and others.

☆ _____. *Mathematical Gems II.* MAA, 1976, 182 pp.
> Fourteen sophisticated essays dealing with a variety of topics, such as graph theory, combinatorial problems, prime numbers, box packing, and others.

☆ _____. *Mathematical Morsels.* MAA, 1978, 249 pp.
> A collection of 91 problems presented in the spirit of *Mathematical Gems I and II.*

Honsberger, Ross, ed. *Mathematical Plums.* MAA, 1979, 182 pp.
> Ten stimulating chapters on such advanced topics as chromatic graphs, Kepler's conics, and Skewes number.

Hughes, Barnabas, Linda Silvey, and Aggie Azzolino. *Mathematics and Humor.* NCTM, 1978, 58 pp.
> Jokes, puns, riddles, cartoons, and so on, many of which make good material for the bulletin board.

☆ Huntley, H. E. *The Divine Proportion: A Study in Mathematical Beauty.* Dover, 1970, 186 pp., paper.

Iglewicz, Boris, and Judith Stoyle. *An Introduction to Mathematical Reasoning.* Macmillan, 1973, 231 pp.
> A readable and adequate survey; exceptionally good exercises.

Infeld, Leopold. *Quest—an Autobiography.* Chelsea, 1980, 361 pp.
> Gives considerable insight into the nature of theoretical physics as it developed in Poland, Britain, Canada, and the United States during the middle of the twentieth century.

Jacobs, Harold R. *Mathematics: A Human Endeavor.* Freeman, 1970, 529 pp.
> Appealing style; excellent presentation for the tyro.

Jacobs, Judith E., ed. *Perspectives on Women and Mathematics.* ERIC, 1978, 165 pp., paper.

Jean, Roger V. *Mathematical Approach to Pattern and Form in Plant Growth.* Wiley, 1984, 222 pp.
> Comprehensive treatment of phyllotaxis and related topics.

Kapur, J. N., ed. *The Nature of Mathematics.* Ram, 1973, 159 pp.
> Stimulating quotations revealing the thoughts and opinions of several hundred mathematicians.

☆ Kasner, Edward, and James R. Newman. *Mathematics and the Imagination.* Simon, 1940, 380 pp.
> Still one of the most popular expositions of mathematics.

Kershner, Richard, and L. R. Wilcox. *Anatomy of Mathematics.* Ronald, 1950, 416 pp.

Khurgin, Ya. *Did You Say Mathematics?* Trans. by George Yankovsky. Import, 1974, 360 pp.
> Informal treatment of selected topics—rubber-sheet mathematics, probability theory, codes, and so forth.

Kim, Scott. *Inversions: A Catalog of Calligraphic Cartwheels.* McGraw, 1980, 200 pp.
> Unique applications of the principles of mathematical symmetry to writing and printing.

Kline, Morris. *Mathematics: A Cultural Approach.* Addison, 1962, 701 pp.

———. *Mathematics and the Search for Knowledge.* Oxford, 1985, 257 pp.

———. *Mathematics: The Loss of Certainty.* Oxford, 1980, 369 pp.
> A history of the philosophy of mathematics, the development of the foundations of mathematics from antiquity to the present, and the relation between mathematics and science; beautifully written, but requires some mathematical maturity.

☆ ———. *Mathematics in the Modern World.* Freeman, 1968, 409 pp.
> Readings from *Scientific American*.

☆ ———. *Mathematics in Western Culture.* Oxford, 1953; Penguin, 1973, 484 pp.

Kline, Morris, ed. *Mathematics: An Introduction to Its Spirit and Use.* Freeman, 1979, 256 pp., cloth and paper.
> Forty selections from *Scientific American;* deals with history, number and algebra, geometry, statistics and probability, symbolic logic, and applications.

Kogelman, Stanley, and Joseph Warren. *Mind over Math.* McGraw, 1979, 256 pp., paper.
> A helpful guide for students who have difficulty with mathematics.

Kramer, Edna E. *The Main Stream of Mathematics.* Oxford, 1951, 321 pp.
> A popular account of the nature, development, and significance of mathematics.

☆ ———. *The Nature and Growth of Modern Mathematics.* Princeton, 1982, 758 pp.
> Pure and applied mathematics; traditional approach integrated with the modern approach; for sophisticated, mature readers.

Lake, Frances, and Joseph Newmark. *Mathematics as a Second Language.* 3d ed. Addison, 1977, 491 pp., paper.

☆ Land, Frank. *The Language of Mathematics.* Doubleday, 1963, 264 pp.

Lieber, Lillian R. *The Education of T. C. Mits.* Illustrated by Hugh G. Lieber. Rev. and enlarged ed. Norton, 1944, 230 pp.
> Unique style and unusual drawings; whimsical yet sober exposition of the fundamental nature of mathematics.

———. *Human Values and Science, Art and Mathematics.* Norton, 1961, 149 pp.

———. *Infinity.* Holt, 1953, 359 pp.

———. *Mits, Wits and Logic.* 3d ed. Norton, 1960, 240 pp.
> Another sparkling and sophisticated exposition.

———. *Take a Number: Mathematics for the Two Billion.* Ronald, 1946, 221 pp.
> A novel introductory survey of elementary algebra and geometry.

☆ Mandelbrot, Benoit B. *The Fractal Geometry of Nature.* Freeman, 1982, 460 pp.
> Absorbing concept of fractal curves and self-replication; for mature readers.

Mathematical Association of America. *Professional Opportunities in Mathematics.* 10th ed. MAA, 1978, 35 pp., paper.
> Completely rewritten and updated; discusses careers in teaching, industry, government, computer science, operations research, statistics, and the actuarial profession.

☆ *Mathematics in the Modern World.* Freeman, 1968, 409 pp.
> Readings from *Scientific American;* an excellent anthology.

☆ Menninger, Karl W. *Mathematics in Your World.* Viking, 1962, 291 pp.

Messick, David M., ed. *Mathematical Thinking in the Behaviorial Sciences.* Freeman, 1968, 231 pp.
> For social science majors, general mathematics students, teachers, nonprofessionals, and so on.

Montague, H. F., and M. D. Montgomery. *The Significance of Mathematics.* Merrill, 1963, 290 pp.

National Council of Teachers of Mathematics. *Applications in School Mathematics.* 1979 Yearbook. NCTM, 1979, 247 pp.
> Nineteen essays ranging from such practical topics as mathematical modeling, statistical inference, and the mathematics of finance to such other areas as symmetry and music.

☆ National Research Council: Committee on Support of Research in the Mathematical Sciences. *The Mathematical Sciences: A Collection of Essays.* MIT, 1969, 271 pp.
> An excellent presentation, for the nonmathematical reader, of some of the outstanding achievements of mid-twentieth-century mathematics; for example, in functional analysis, probability theory, combinatorics, transfinite numbers, mathematical linguistics and computers, and so on.

Newman, James R., ed. *The World of Mathematics.* 4 vols. Simon, 1956, 2535 pp.
> A comprehensive anthology of assorted readings about many facets of mathematics from ancient times to the present.

☆ Newsom, Carroll V. *Mathematical Discourses: The Heart of Mathematical Science.* Prentice, 1964, 121 pp.
> Sophisticated and scholarly exposition of mathematical thought; for mature readers.

☆ Ogilvy, Charles Stanley. *Through the Mathescope.* Oxford, 1965, 162 pp.
> Popular essays on number theory, algebra, geometry, and elementary analysis.

———. *Tomorrow's Math: Unsolved Problems for the Amateur.* Oxford, 1972, 198 pp.

Osen, Lynn M. *Women in Mathematics.* MIT, 1974, 185 pp.

☆ Page, Warren, ed. *Two-Year College Mathematics Readings.* MAA, 1981, 304 pp.
> Collection of forty-five stimulating articles.

☆ Pedoe, Dan. *The Gentle Art of Mathematics.* Macmillan, 1959; Dover, 1973, 143 pp.
> Delightfully readable informal discussions of number scales, probability, infinity, logic, topology, and other topics.

☆ Penney, David E. *Perspectives in Mathematics*. Benjamin, 1972, 349 pp.
> An expository treatment, similar to Stein's *Mathematics: the Man-Made Universe*, only somewhat more penetrating and sophisticated; numerous exercises, but good collateral reading.

Perl, Teri. *Math Equals: Biographies of Women Mathematicians + Related Activities*. Addison, 1978, 250 pp. paper.
> Discusses the lives of nine famous women mathematicians and gives examples of their contributions; chief emphasis is on the obstacles each woman overcame.

☆ Péter, Rózsa. *Playing with Infinity: Mathematical Explorations and Excursions*. Translated by Z. P. Dienes. Dover, 1976, 268 pp., paper.
> Popular treatment of number theory, Galois theory, geometry, calculus, symbolic logic. Gödel's theorem, and so on; reprint of 1962 edition.

Rademacher, Hans. *Higher Mathematics from an Elementary Point of View*. Edited by D. Goldfield. Birkhauser, 1983, 138 pp.
> Companion volume to the author's earlier book, *The Enjoyment of Mathematics*.

☆ Rademacher, Hans, and Otto Toeplitz. *The Enjoyment of Mathematics: Selections from Mathematics for the Amateur*. Princeton, 1957, 204 pp.
> Fairly advanced but thoroughly readable essays on significant topics.

Rapport, Samuel, and Helen Wright, eds. *Mathematics*. Washington, 1964, 319 pp., paper.
> A diversified anthology of essays and excerpts on the nature of mathematics and its role in our civilization.

Rashevsky, Nicolas. *Looking at History through Mathematics*. MIT, 1968, 199 pp.
> Possible applications of the mathematics of growing organisms to the growth of societies over long periods of time.

Reichmann, W. J. *The Spell of Mathematics*. Methuen, 1967; B. and N., 1968, 272 pp.

Renyi, Alfred. *Dialogues on Mathematics*. Holden, 1967, 100 pp.
> Discussion of the nature of mathematics and its applications.

Rosen, Joe. *Symmetry Discovered*. Cambridge, 1975, 138 pp.
> Excellent bibliography.

Rucker, Rudy. *Infinity and the Mind: The Science and Philosophy of the Infinite*. Birkhauser, 1982, 342 pp.
> Introduction to transfinite cardinals; for mature readers.

Runion, Garth E. *The Golden Section and Related Curiosa*. Scott, 1972, 150 pp.

Saaty, Thomas L., and F. J. Weyl, eds. *The Spirit and the Uses of the Mathematical Sciences*. McGraw, 1969, 301 pp.

Sawyer, W. W. *A Path to Modern Mathematics*. Penguin, 1966, 224 pp., paper.

——. *The Search for Pattern*. Penguin, 1970, 349 pp., paper.
: Insight into mathematical ideas; for students and nonspecialists.

Schoenberg, Isaac J. *Mathematical Time Exposures*. MAA, 1982, 270 pp., cloth/softbound.
: Interesting collection of independent essays reminiscent of Hugo Steinhaus's *Mathematical Snapshots*.

Selkirk, K. E. *Pattern and Place: An Introduction to the Mathematics of Geography*. Cambridge, 1982, 203 pp., paper.
: Excellent; high school and college level.

Singh, Jagjit. *Great Ideas of Modern Mathematics: Their Nature and Use*. Dover, 1959, 312 pp., paper.

☆ Smith, Karl J. *The Nature of Modern Mathematics*. Brooks, 1980, 620 pp.
: Well-written exposition for students, teachers, and the general reader.

Smith, Steven B. *The Great Mental Calculators: The Psychology, Methods, and Lives of Calculating Prodigies, Past and Present*. Columbia, 1983, 374 pp.
: Comprehensive and definitive.

Solow, Daniel. *How to Read and Do Proofs: An Introduction to Mathematical Thought Processes*. Wiley, 1982, 172 pp., softbound.

Spitznagel, Edward L., Jr. *Selected Topics in Mathematics*. Holt, 1971, 323 pp.
: Fairly sophisticated level.

Steen, Lynn Arthur. *Mathematics Tomorrow*. Springer, 1981, 250 pp.
: Thought-provoking essays addressed to mathematics teachers.

Steen, Lynn Arthur, ed. *Mathematics Today: Twelve Informal Essays*. Random, 1980, 367 pp.
: Intriguing essays on the cultural relevance of contemporary mathematics, touching on conventional, theoretical, and applied mathematics; a good answer to the question "What do mathematicians do?"

☆ Stein, Sherman K. *Mathematics, the Man-Made Universe: An Introduction to the Spirit of Mathematics*. 3d ed. Freeman, 1976, 573 pp.
: Original and stimulating.

☆ Steinhaus, Hugo. *Mathematical Snapshots*. 3d American ed. Oxford, 1983, 311 pp., softbound.

Tietze, Heinrich. *Famous Problems of Mathematics: Solved and Unsolved Mathematical Problems from Antiquity to Modern Times*. 2d ed. Graylock, 1965, 367 pp.
: Scholarly discussion of miscellaneous significant problems, including space curvature, infinity, prime numbers, angle trisection, circle squaring, regular polygon of seventeen sides, four-color problem, and so on. For mature readers.

Townsend, M. Stewart. *Mathematics in Sport*. Wiley, 1984, 202 pp., softbound.
: Covers a wide variety of sports; involves mathematics through calculus.

☆ Valens, Evans G., Jr. *The Number of Things: Pythagoras, Geometry and Humming Strings.* Dutton, 1964, 189 pp.
   Pythagorean philosophy of numbers, including the golden section, the Pythagorean theorem, tangrams and dissections, musical scales, and related topics.

☆ Wilder, Raymond L. *Mathematics as a Cultural System.* Pergamon, 1981, 182 pp.

Willerding, Margaret F., and Ruth A. Hayward. *Mathematics: The Alphabet of Science.* Wiley, 1968, 285 pp.
   Simple treatment of significant topics to illustrate the scope and beauty of mathematics.

Young, Frederick H. *The Nature of Mathematics.* Wiley, 1968, 407 pp.

Youse, Bevan K. *An Introduction to Mathematics.* Allyn, 1970, 287 pp.
   An introduction to the nature and spirit of mathematics.

☆ Zippin, Leo. *Uses of Infinity.* New Mathematical Library, vol. 7. Random, 1962, 151 pp., cloth and paper.

Foundations and Philosophy of Mathematics; Logic

Barker, Stephen F. *Philosophy of Mathematics.* Prentice, 1964, 111 pp., paper.
   For the mature reader.

Benacerraf, Paul, and Hilary Putnam, eds. *Philosophy of Mathematics: Selected Readings.* Prentice, 1964, 536 pp.
   Rather steep reading, but includes rewarding selections by von Neumann, Hempel, Poincaré, Frege, Russell, Hilbert, Carnap, Quine, and others. Extensive bibliography. For the advanced student.

Brant, Vincent, and Marvin Keedy. *Elementary Logic for Secondary Schools.* Holt, 1962, 123 pp., paper.

☆ Davis, Philip, and Reuben Hersh. *The Mathematical Experience.* Birkhauser, 1981, 440 pp.
   Essays on the history, nature, and philosophy of mathematics; for mature readers.

☆ Eves, Howard, and Carroll V. Newsom. *An Introduction to the Foundations and Fundamental Concepts of Mathematics.* Rev. ed. Holt, 1965, 398 pp.
   An advanced text; comprehensive and rigorous.

Gensler, Harry J. *Godel's Theorem Simplified.* University, 1984, 83 pp., cloth and paper.
   Understandable, but for mature readers.

Goodstein, Reuben L. *Mathematical Logic.* Ungar, 1961, 104 pp.

Gradshteyn, I. S. *Direct and Converse Theorems: The Elements of Symbolic Logic.* Pergamon, 1963, 173 pp.

Halberstadt, William H. *An Introduction to Modern Logic.* Harper, 1960, 221 pp.
:   An elementary textbook on symbolic logic.

☆ Kenelly, John W. *Informal Logic.* Allyn, 1967, 134 pp.
:   An introduction to symbolic logic; presupposes familiarity with high school algebra; bibliography.

Kitcher, Philip. *The Nature of Mathematical Knowledge.* Oxford, 1983, 287 pp.
:   Philosophical; rather technical; for sophisticated readers.

Körner, Stephan. *The Philosophy of Mathematics.* Harper, 1960, 198 pp., paper.
:   An introductory treatment, but nonetheless scholarly and substantial; for mature readers.

☆ Meschkowski, Herbert. *Evolution of Mathematical Thought.* Holden, 1965, 157 pp.
:   Scholarly historical introduction to the foundations of mathematics; also of general cultural, philosophical, and pedagogical interest.

Nagel, Ernest, and James Newman. *Godel's Proof.* NYU, 1958, 118 pp., cloth and paper.
:   An exceptionally lucid explanation of an abstruse topic; for the mathematically mature reader.

Smith, Karl J. *Introduction to Symbolic Logic.* Brooks, 1974, 119 pp.
:   A good introductory survey of the subject.

Smullyan, Raymond. *Five Thousand B.C. and Other Philosophical Fantasies.* St. Martin's 1983, 224 pp.

☆ Sondheimer, E., and A. Rogerson. *Numbers and Infinity: Historical Account of Mathematical Concepts.* Cambridge, 1981, 172 pp.
:   Emphasis on foundations and philosophy.

Stoll, R. R. *Sets, Logic, and Axiomatic Theories.* Freeman, 1961, 206 pp., paper.
:   Elementary, but fairly rigorous.

☆ Suppes, Patrick. *Introduction to Logic.* Van Nostrand, 1957, 312 pp.
:   College level.

Waismann, Friedrich. *Introduction to Mathematical Thinking.* Harper, 1959, 260 pp., paper.
:   Logical foundations of mathematics; for advanced readers.

☆ Wilder, Raymond L. *Introduction to the Foundations of Mathematics.* 3d ed. Krieger, 1980, 346 pp.
:   For advanced students, emphasizes set theory and logic.

History and Cultural Evolution of Mathematics

Aaboe, Asger. *Episodes from the Early History of Mathematics.* New Mathematical Library, vol. 13. Random, 1964, 133 pp., cloth and paper.
  Babylonian mathematics; early Greek mathematicians; Archimedes and Ptolemy.

Ball, W. W. R. *A Short Account of the History of Mathematics.* 4th ed. Dover, 1960, 522 pp., paper.

Beckmann, Petr. *A History of Pi (π).* St. Martin's, 1976, 200 pp., paper.
  Delightful account of the history of mathematics and of the history of π in particular.

Bell, E. T. *The Development of Mathematics.* 2d ed. McGraw, 1945, 583 pp.
  Advanced reading; authoritative; brings history down to the early twentieth century.

Berger, Melvin. *For Good Measure: The Story of Modern Measurement.* McGraw, 1969, 160 pp.

Boyer, Carl B. *History of Analytic Geometry.* Academic, 1956, 291 pp.

———. *The History of the Calculus and Its Conceptual Development.* Dover, 1959, 346 pp., paper.
  Scholarly treatise on the historical development of the calculus from earliest times to the present.

☆ ———. *History of Mathematics.* Wiley, 1968, 717 pp.
  Excellent survey of the subject.

Bunt, Lucas N. H., Phillip S. Jones, and Jack D. Bedient. *The Historical Roots of Elementary Mathematics.* Prentice, 1976, 299 pp.
  A very readable introduction to the subject.

Burton, David M. *The History of Mathematics: An Introduction.* Allyn, 1985, 678 pp.
  Very readable; 19th and 20th centuries only briefly developed.

Calinger, Ronald, ed. *Classics of Mathematics.* Moore, 1982, 742 pp., softbound.
  An unusual sourcebook on the history of mathematics; much new material.

Cohen, Patricia C. *A Calculating People: The Spread of Numeracy in Early America.* Chicago, 1982, 270 pp.

☆ Dantzig, Tobias. *The Bequest of the Greeks.* Allen, 1955; Greenwood, 1969, 191 pp.
  Very scholarly; quite readable.

Dedron, P., and J. Itard. *Mathematics and Mathematicians.* 2 vols. Translated by J. V. Field. Transworld, 1973, 325 pp., 222 pp.
  Scholarly presentation of pre-nineteenth-century mathematics in nontechnical language.

☆ Eves, Howard. *Great Moments in Mathematics (before 1650).* MAA, 1980, 270 pp.
  A fascinating overview of the history of mathematics to 1650, dramatically told.

☆ ——— . *Great Moments in Mathematics (after 1650)*. MAA, 1981, 263 pp.
    A welcome sequel to the earlier volume of *Great Moments*, bringing the story up to date.

☆ ——— . *An Introduction to the History of Mathematics*. 5th ed., rev. and enlarged. Saunders, 1983, 593 pp.

Farrington, Benjamin. *Greek Science*. Penguin, 1961, 320 pp., paper.
    Very readable, especially chapter 3, part 1, and chapter 2, part 2.

Freebury, H. A. *A History of Mathematics*. Macmillan, 1961, 198 pp.

Gillings, Richard J. *Mathematics in the Time of the Pharaohs*. MIT, 1972, 286 pp.

Gittleman, Arthur. *History of Mathematics*. Merrill, 1975, 291 pp.

Heath, Thomas L. *Diophantus of Alexandria*. 2d rev. ed. Dover, 1964, 387 pp., paper; Smith, 1964, cloth.

——— . *A Manual of Greek Mathematics*. Dover, 1931, 552 pp., paper.

Hofmann, Joseph E. *Classical Mathematics: A Concise History of the Classical Era in Mathematics*. Philosophical, 1959, 159 pp.

——— . *The History of Mathematics*. Philosophical, 1957, 132 pp.

Hogben, Lancelot. *Mathematics in the Making*. Doubleday, 1960, 320 pp.
    Colorful and attractive, even if slightly superficial.

Karpinski, L. C. *The History of Arithmetic*. Russell, 1965, 200 pp.

☆ Kline, Morris. *Mathematical Thought from Ancient to Modern Times*. Oxford, 1972, 1238 pp.
    A classic, scholarly work; comprehensive, lucid, and perceptive; major emphasis on mathematical developments since the seventeenth century; for sophisticated readers, for both study and reference.

☆ Kramer, Edna E. *The Nature and Growth of Modern Mathematics*. Princeton, 1981, 758 pp., paper.
    Charming and stimulating historical survey.

Lanczos, Cornelius. *Space through the Ages*. Academic, 1970, 320 pp.
    A history of geometrical thinking; for the sophisticated reader.

Lasserre, François. *The Birth of Mathematics in the Age of Plato*. Meridian, 1966, 190 pp., paper.

Linn, Charles F., ed. *The Ages of Mathematics*. 4 vols. Doubleday, 1977.
Vol. 1—*The Origins*. Michal Moffatt. 137 pp.
Vol. 2—*Mathematics East and West*. Charles Linn. 151 pp.
Vol. 3—*Western Mathematics Comes of Age*. Cynthia Cook. 151 pp.
Vol. 4—*The Modern Ages*. Peter Cook. 137 pp.
    For young people; very readable.

Maziarz, Edward A., and Thomas Greenwood. *Greek Mathematical Philosophy.* Ungar, 1968, 271 pp.
: A cultural survey of the period from Thales through Euclid.

Menninger, Karl. *Number Words and Number Symbols: A Cultural History of Numbers.* MIT, 1969, 480 pp.

☆ Meschkowski, Herbert. *Evolution of Mathematical Thought.* Holden, 1965, 157 pp.
: For mature readers; scholarly and sophisticated.

☆ ———. *Ways of Thought of Great Mathematicians.* Holden, 1964, 110 pp., paper.
: Excellent supplement to conventional histories of mathematics; surveys the creative thinking of the Pythagoreans, Nicholas of Cusa, Pascal, Gauss, Boole, Weierstrass, and Cantor.

Midonick, Henrietta O., ed. *The Treasury of Mathematics.* Philosophical, 1965, 820 pp.
: Collection of over fifty essays on significant contributions in the historical development of mathematics.

Mikami, Yoshio. *The Development of Mathematics in China and Japan.* 2d ed. Chelsea, 1974, 389 pp.
: Reprint of the 1913 edition.

Mitchell, Merle. *Mathematical History: Activities, Puzzles, Stories, and Games.* NCTM, 1978, 74 pp.
: Appropriate for grades 4–6 and up.

Morgan, Bryan. *Men and Discoveries in Mathematics.* Murray, 1972, 235 pp.

☆ National Council of Teachers of Mathematics. *Historical Topics for the Mathematics Classroom.* 31st Yearbook. NCTM, 1969, 544 pp.
: A substantial treatment of the use of the history of mathematics in the teaching of mathematics. Significant historical material presented in a form designed specifically for classroom use.

Neugebauer, Otto. *The Exact Sciences in Antiquity.* 2d ed. Harper, 1962, 240 pp., paper.
: A scholarly classic.

Owen, George E. *The Universe of the Mind.* Hopkins, 1971, 349 pp.
: A history of ideas in mathematics and physics.

Popp, Walter. *History of Mathematics: Topics for Schools.* Translated from the German by Maxim Bruckheimer. Transworld, 1975, 150 pp.

Resnikoff, H. L., and R. O. Wells, Jr. *Mathematics in Civilization.* Preliminary ed. Holt, 1973, 372 pp.
: Historical development of people's "ability to compute" and the "geometrical nature of space"; bibliography.

Ruchlis, Hy, and Jack Engelhardt. *The Story of Mathematics.* Bailey, 1972, 148 pp.
: For young readers.

☆ Sanford, Vera. *A Short History of Mathematics*. Houghton, 1930, 402 pp.

☆ Schaaf, William L. *Mathematics and Science: An Adventure in Postage Stamps*. NCTM, 1978, 152 pp., paper.
: A popular account of the history of mathematics and science from ancient times to the present as told through postage stamps.

☆ Scott, Joseph F. *A History of Mathematics from Antiquity to the Beginning of the Nineteenth Century*. 2d ed., International Publications, 1960; B. and N., 1970, 266 pp.

Smith, David Eugene. *History of Mathematics*. 2 vols. Dover, vol. 1, 1923, vol. 2, 1925; 596 pp., 725 pp., paper.

———. *A Source Book in Mathematics*. 1929. Reprint. 2 vols. Dover, 1959.

Smith, David Eugene, and Jekuthiel Ginsburg. *History of Mathematics in America before 1900*. MAA Carus Monographs, no. 5. Open, 1934, 209 pp.

☆ Struik, D. J. *A Concise History of Mathematics*. 3d rev. ed. Dover, 1967, 299 pp., paper.

———. *A Source Book in Mathematics, 1200–1800*. Harvard, 1969, 430 pp.

Sullivan, J. W. N. *The History of Mathematics in Europe*. Oxford, 1925, 109 pp.

Turnbull, H. W. *The Mathematical Discoveries of Newton*. Blackie, 1945, 68 pp.

☆ Van der Waerden, B. L. *Geometry and Algebra in Ancient Civilizations*. Springer, 1982, 233 pp.
: A fascinating book that deepens our insight concerning the earliest origins of mathematics.

☆ ———. *Science Awakening*. Oxford, 1961, 306 pp.; Wiley, paper.
: A scholarly and comprehensive treatment of Babylonian, Egyptian, and Greek mathematics.

☆ Wilder, Raymond L. *Evolution of Mathematical Concepts*. Taylor, 1978, 240 pp., paper.
: A perceptive and engaging book; for mature readers.

☆ Wolff, Peter. *Breakthroughs in Mathematics*. New American, 1964, 285 pp., paper.
: A vivid presentation of the significant contributions made by nine great mathematicians: Euclid, Lobachevski, Descartes, Archimedes, Dedekind, Russell, Euler, Laplace, and Boole.

☆ Zaslavsky, Claudia. *Africa Counts*. Prindle, 1973, 328 pp.
: A unique contribution to mathematics history and to black cultural anthropology; includes, among other topics, recreations and numerology.

Biographies and Personalities

☆ Albers, Donald J., and G. L. Alexanderson, eds. *Mathematical People*. Birkhauser, 1984, 260 pp.
   Delightful biographical sketches of contemporary mathematicians.

Andrade, E. N. da C. *Sir Isaac Newton*. Doubleday, 1958, 111 pp., paper.

Anthony, H. D. *Sir Isaac Newton*. Abelard, 1960; Collier, 1961, 188 pp., paper.

Armitage, Angus. *Copernicus: The Founder of Modern Astronomy*. Barnes, 1962, paper.

———. *The World of Copernicus*. Mentor, 1951, 165 pp., paper.
   Reprint of *Sun, Stand Thou Still* (Abelard, 1947).

Beckhard, Arthur. *Albert Einstein*. Putnam, 1959, 126 pp.; Avon, 1960, paper.

☆ Bell, Eric T. *Men of Mathematics*. Simon, 1937, 592 pp., cloth and paper.
   A classic; contains piquant, terse characterizations of the personalities and achievements of some thirty-five outstanding mathematicians of all time.

☆ Bernstein, Jeremy. *Einstein*. Edited by Frank Kermode. Viking, 1973, 242 pp., cloth and paper.
   Unpretentious, simple exposition; perceptive and accurate account of what Einstein did and what kind of person he was.

Bishop, Morris. *Pascal: The Life of Genius*. Williams, 1936, 398 pp.

Bixby, William, and Giorgio DeSantillano. *The Universe of Galileo and Newton*. Harper, 1964, 153 pp.

Bühler, W. K. *Gauss: A Biographical Study*. Springer, 1981, 208 pp.
   For mature readers.

☆ Cahn, William. *Einstein: A Pictorial Biography*. Citadel, 1955, 128 pp., paper.

Cailliet, Emile. *Pascal, the Emergence of Genius*. Harper, 1961, 383 pp.

Calinger, Ronald. *Gottfried Wilhelm Leibniz*. Rensselaer, 1976, 102 pp., paper.

Caspar, Max. *Kepler: 1571–1630*. Collier, 1962, 416 pp., paper; Abelard, 1962.

Christianson, Gale E. *In the Presence of the Creator: Isaac Newton and His Times*. Free, 1984, 608 pp.

Cooke, Roger. *The Mathematics of Sonya Kovalevskaya*. Springer, 1984, 234 pp.
   Biography with chief emphasis on Kovalevski's contributions to mathematics.

Coolidge, Julian. *The Mathematics of Great Amateurs*. Dover, 1949, 211 pp., paper.

Dijksterhuis, E. J. *Archimedes.* Humanities, 1957, 421 pp.

Dreyer, J. L. E. *Tycho Brahe.* Dover, 1963, 405 pp., paper; Smith, 1964, cloth.
   A picture of science in the sixteenth century.

☆ Dukas, Helen, and Banesh Hoffmann. *Albert Einstein: The Human Side.* Princeton, 1979, 167 pp.
   Selections from Einstein's writings.

Dunnington, G. Waldo. *Carl Friedrich Gauss: Titan of Science.* Hafner, 1955, 479 pp.
   A definitive biography; scholarly and exhaustive.

Einstein, Albert. *Out of My Later Years.* Philosophical, 1950, 282 pp.
   Collected essays by Einstein, revealing his political, social, and philosophical attitudes as well as observations on science.

Fermi, Laura, and Gilberto Bernardini. *Galileo and the Scientific Revolution.* Basic, 1961, 150 pp.; Fawcett, paper.

Frank, Phillip. *Einstein: His Life and Times.* Knopf, 1953, 298 pp.

Freeman, Mae B. *The Story of Albert Einstein.* Random, 1958, 178 pp.

☆ French, A. P., ed. *Einstein: A Centenary Volume.* Harvard, 1979, 322 pp.
   An impressive collection of writing by, and about, Einstein, covering nearly all his life and work.

Halacy, Dan. *Charles Babbage: Father of the Computer.* Crowell, 1970, 170 pp.

Hall, Tord. *Carl Friedrich Gauss: A Biography.* Translated by Albert Froderberg. MIT, 1970, 176 pp.
   A sophisticated treatment with major emphasis on Gauss's contributions to mathematics.

Heath, Thomas L. *Diophantus of Alexandria.* 2d rev. ed. Dover, 1964, 387 pp., paper; Smith, 1964, cloth.

Heisenberg, Elisabeth. *Inner Exile: Recollections of a Life with Werner Heisenberg.* Birkhauser, 1984, 144 pp.

Hoffman, Banesh, and Helen Dukas. *Albert Einstein: Creator and Rebel.* Viking, 1972, 272 pp.
   A very perceptive biography.

Infeld, Leopold. *Albert Einstein.* Scribner, 1950, 134 pp., cloth and paper.

———. *Whom the Gods Love: The Story of Evariste Galois.* Classics in Mathematics Education series, vol. 7. NCTM, 1978, 323 pp.
   A reprint of the original 1948 edition.

Kennedy, Don H. *Little Sparrow: A Portrait of Sophia Kovalevsky.* Ohio, 1983, 341 pp., cloth/softbound.

Knight, David C. *Isaac Newton: Mastermind of Modern Science.* Watts, 1961, 153 pp.
   For young readers.

———. *Johannes Kepler and Planetary Motion.* Watts, 1962, 186 pp.
   For young readers.

☆ Koblitz, Ann H. *A Convergence of Lives: Sofia Kovalevskaia, Scientist, Writer, and Revolutionary.* Birkhauser, 1983, 305 pp.
   A warm and sympathetic biography.

Kovalevskaya, S. *A Russian Childhood.* Translated by Beatrice Stillman. Springer, 1978, 250 pp.
   An enjoyable biographical memoir with emphasis on Kovalevski's early years.

Leerburger, Benedict. *Josiah Gibbs, American Theoretical Physicist.* Watts, 1963, 118 pp.
   For young readers.

Levinger, Elma E. *Albert Einstein.* Messner, 1949, 174 pp.
   Popular, informal style.

———. *Galileo: First Observer of Marvelous Things.* Messner, 1952, 180 pp.
   Popular, informal style.

Lowe, V. *Alfred North Whitehead.* Hopkins, 1985, 351 pp.

McMullin, Ernan, ed. *Galileo: Man of Science.* Basic, 1967, 455 pp.
   A collection of twenty-three papers by distinguished scholars; bibliography.

Manuel, Frank E. *A Portrait of Isaac Newton.* Harvard, 1968, 478 pp.

Marcus, Rebecca. *Galileo and Experimental Science.* Watts, 1961, 134 pp.
   For young readers.

Michelmore, Peter. *Einstein: Profile of the Man.* Dodd, 1962, 269 pp.; Apollo, 1963, paper.

Moore, Patrick. *Isaac Newton.* Putnam, 1958, 128 pp.

More, Louis T. *Isaac Newton: A Biography.* Smith, 1963, 673 pp.

☆ Muir, Jane. *Of Men and Numbers: The Story of the Great Mathematicians.* Dodd, 1961, 249 pp.; Dell, paper.
   Lucid and crisp accounts.

Ore, Oystein. *Cardano, the Gambling Scholar.* Smith, 1953, 249 pp.; Dover, paper.

———. *Niels Henrik Abel, Mathematician Extraordinary.* Chelsea, 1974, 277 pp.

Osen, Lynn M. *Women in Mathematics.* MIT, 1975, 185 pp.

Peare, Catherine O. *Albert Einstein.* Holt, 1949, 152 pp.

Perl, Teri. *Math Equals: Biographies of Women Mathematicians and Related Activities.* Addison, 1978, 250 pp., paper.
   Fairly advanced treatment, but the biographical material is interesting; Hypatia, du Châtelet, Agnesi, Germain, Somerville, Lovelace, Kovalevskaya, Young, Noether.

Reid, Constance. *Hilbert.* Springer, 1970, 290 pp.

Ronan, Colin. *The Astronomers.* Hill, 1964, 232 pp.
> The lives, beliefs, and discoveries of such pioneers as Pythagoras, Copernicus, Newton, and Einstein, among others.

☆ Schaaf, William L. *Carl Friedrich Gauss, Prince of Mathematicians.* Watts, 1964, 168 pp.
> For young readers.

Sootin, Harry. *Isaac Newton.* Messner, 1955, 191 pp.
> Suitable for young readers.

Stonaker, Frances B. *Famous Mathematicians.* Lippincott, 1967, 118 pp.
> Simple treatment, at junior high school level, of Euclid, Archimedes, al-Khwarismi, Descartes, Newton, Lagrange, Gauss, Galois, von Neumann, and Wiener.

☆ Sullivan, J. W. N. *Isaac Newton: 1642–1727.* Macmillan, 1938, 275 pp.
> Very readable, penetrating study; one of the best biographies of Newton.

Tannenbaum, Beulah, and Myra Stillman. *Isaac Newton: Pioneer in Space Mathematics.* McGraw, 1959, 128 pp.

☆ Turnbull, H. W. *The Great Mathematicians.* NYU, 1961, 141 pp.; Simon, 1962, paper.
> Excellent accounts of Pythagoras, Euclid, Archimedes, Descartes, Newton, Euler, Lagrange, Gauss, and others.

Vallentin, Antonina. *The Drama of Albert Einstein.* Doubleday, 1954, 312 pp.
> A very warm and human account.

Wheeler, L. P. *Josiah Willard Gibbs: The History of a Great Mind.* Yale, 1952, 270 pp.

Whitrow, G. J., ed. *Einstein: The Man and His Achievement.* Dover, 1967, 1973, 94 pp., paper.
> The text of a series of BBC radio programs; major emphasis on Einstein's personality and his impact on friends and fellow scientists; informal, authoritative; bibliography,

Weiner, Norbert. *I Am a Mathematician.* Doubleday, 1956, 380 pp., cloth; MIT, paper.
> Autobiography of a well-known mathematician and former child prodigy; for mature readers.

Science and Mathematics

☆ Adler, Irving. *The Changing Tools of Science: From Yardstick to Synchrotron.* Day, 1973, 158 pp.
> Revision of the 1958 edition; emphasis on the concepts of precision and approximation.

_____. *The Elementary Mathematics of the Atom.* Day, 1965, 160 pp.

☆ Ahrendt, Myrl H. *The Mathematics of Space Exploration.* Holt, 1965, 160 pp., cloth and paper.

Barnett, Lincoln. *The Universe and Dr. Einstein.* New American, 1950, 140 pp., paper; 2d rev. ed., Harper, 1957, paper.

Bitter, Francis. *Mathematical Aspects of Physics: An Introduction.* Doubleday, 1963, 188 pp., paper.
Semitechnical; data gathering; analysis of data; design of experiments. Very readable.

Bochner, S. *The Role of Mathematics in the Rise of Science.* Princeton, 1966.
For mature readers.

☆ Burger, Dionys. *Sphereland: A Fantasy about Curved Spaces and an Expanding Universe.* Crowell, 1965, 220 pp.

Calder, Nigel. *Einstein's Universe.* Viking, 1979, 154 pp.
Emphasis on the theory of relativity.

☆ Cohen, I. Bernard. *Revolution in Science.* Harvard, 1985, 711 pp.
Authoritative and illuminating.

Coleman, James A. *Relativity for the Layman.* Frederick, 1958, 131 pp.; New American, paper.
A very readable account; includes historical backgrounds.

☆ Dantzig, Tobias. *Aspects of Science.* Macmillan, 1937, 285 pp.

Drake, Stillman. *Galileo at Work: His Scientific Biography.* Chicago, 1981, 536 pp.

Friedrichs, K. O. *From Pythagoras to Einstein.* Random, 1966, 88 pp., paper.

Gamow, George. *One, Two, Three . . . Infinity.* Rev. ed. Viking, 1961, 340 pp., cloth and paper.
Inviting discussion of significant ideas in mathematics and science.

☆ Gardner, Martin. *The Ambidextrous Universe: Asymmetry and Time-Reversed Worlds.* 2d rev. ed. Scribner, 1979, 293 pp.
Stimulating discussion of left-right symmetry, asymmetry in nature, crystals and molecules, fourth dimension, parity, and related topics.

☆ ――――. *The Relativity Explosion.* Vintage, 1976, 198 pp.
A revised and updated edition of *Relativity for the Millions:* excellent illustrations and exposition; minimum of mathematics.

――――. *Space Puzzles.* Bell, 1975, 96 pp.
Subtitled *Curious Questions and Answers about the Solar System,* the book leans more toward physics than mathematics; it is, however, replete with information and stimulating questions.

Grossman, Stanley I., and James E. Turner. *Mathematics for the Biological Sciences.* Macmillan, 1974, 526 pp.

Hawkins, David. *The Language of Nature: An Essay in the Philosophy of Science.* Freeman, 1964, 372 pp.
<blockquote>Scholarly and stimulating; excellent chapters on the nature of number, geometry, analysis, measurement, and probability; for mature readers.</blockquote>

☆ Hooke, Robert, and Douglas Shaffer. *Math and Aftermath.* Walker, 1965, 233 pp.

mathematics by creating models; for mature readers.
<blockquote>How the applied mathematician bridges the gap between physical reality and</blockquote>

Infeld, Leopold. *Albert Einstein: His Work and Its Influence on Our World.* Scribner, 1950, 132 pp., cloth and paper.

☆ Kline, Morris. *Mathematics and the Physical World.* Crowell, 1959, 482 pp.
<blockquote>An illuminating survey of the relation of mathematics to science.</blockquote>

Kondo, Herbert. *Adventures in Space and Time: The Story of Relativity.* Holiday, 1966, 93 pp.

Lanczos, Cornelius. *Albert Einstein and the Cosmic World Order.* Interscience, 1965, 139 pp.
<blockquote>For mature readers.</blockquote>

Landau, L. D., and G. B. Rumer. *What Is Relativity?* Basic, 1961, 72 pp.
<blockquote>Suitable for grades 9–12.</blockquote>

Levi, Primo. *The Periodic Table.* Schocken, 1984, 160 pp.

Lieber, Lillian R. *The Einstein Theory of Relativity.* Illustrated by Hugo G. Lieber. Holt, 1945, 324 pp.
<blockquote>Unusual and lucid popular explanation; excellent for the amateur.</blockquote>

Marriott, F. H. C. *Basic Mathematics for the Biological and Social Sciences.* Pergamon, 1970, 229 pp.

Nevanlinna, Rolf. *Space, Time and Relativity.* Translated from the German by Gordon Reece. Addison, 1968, 158 pp.
<blockquote>Excellent exposition; highly recommended.</blockquote>

☆ Newman, James R. *Science and Sensibility.* 2 vols. Simon, 1961. Abridged ed., Doubleday (Anchor), 1963, 541 pp., paper.
<blockquote>Thoughts about the contributions of scientists and philosophers over the centuries; slightly verbose, but perceptive and provocative; for mature readers.</blockquote>

Owen, George E. *Fundamentals of Scientific Mathematics.* Hopkins, 1961, 274 pp.; Harper, paper.

Polya, George. *Mathematical Methods in Science.* MAA, 1977, 234 pp.

Rucker, Rudolf v. B. *Geometry, Relativity and the Fourth Dimension.* Dover, 1977, 133 pp., paper.
<blockquote>Basic concepts of time and space; intuitive approach reminiscent of Edwin Abbott's *Flatland*; annotated bibliography.</blockquote>

☆ Schaaf, William L. *Mathematics and Science: An Adventure in Postage Stamps.* NCTM, 1978, 152 pp., paper.
>A popular account of the influence of mathematics on science and technology.

☆ Schiffer, M. M., and L. Bowden. *The Role of Mathematics in Science.* MAA, 1984, 207 pp., softbound.
>Discusses growth, time, optics, motion, energy; for mature readers.

Schwartz, Jacob T. *Relativity in Illustrations.* NYU, 1962, 117 pp.

Silverberg, Robert. *Men Who Mastered the Atom.* Putnam, 1965, 193 pp.

Smith, J. Maynard. *Mathematical Ideas in Biology.* Cambridge, 1968, 152 pp.

Stephenson, G. *Mathematical Methods for Science Students.* Longmans, 1973, 528 pp.

Struble, Mitch. *The Web of Space-Time: A Step by Step Approach to Relativity.* Westminster, 1973, 174 pp.

Wells, Alexander F. *The Third Dimension in Chemistry.* Oxford, 1956, 148 pp.
>Application of geometry to molecular structure; transformations of rotation, translation, and reflection; sophisticated treatment.

Weyl, Hermann. *Philosophy of Mathematics and Natural Science.* Princeton, 1949, 311 pp.; Atheneum, 1963, paper.

Whitaker, E. T. *From Euclid to Eddington.* Dover, 1959, 224 pp., paper.

Recreational Mathematics

Abraham, R. M. *Diversions and Pastimes.* Smith, 1935, 153 pp.; Dover, 1964, paper.
>Match and coin games; knots and strings; games with paper; conventional puzzles.

☆ Bakst, Aaron. *Mathematical Puzzles and Pastimes.* 2d ed. Van Nostrand, 1965, 242 pp.
>A collection of more or less conventional mathematical recreations.

Ball, W. W. R. *Mathematical Recreations and Essays.* Macmillan, 1960, 418 pp., cloth and paper.
>Exceedingly popular; contains most of the classical arithmetic and geometric recreations; also polyhedrons, chessboard recreations, magic squares, map-coloring problems, classical problems of antiquity, cryptography.

☆ Ball, W. W. R., and H. S. M. Coxeter. *Mathematical Recreations and Essays.* 12th ed. Toronto, 1974, 428 pp.
>An updated edition of a well-known classic; contains several new sections.

Bandelow, Christoph. *Inside Rubik's Cube and Beyond.* Birkhauser, 1982, 125 pp., softbound.

Barnard, Douglas St. Paul. *Adventures in Mathematics.* Hawthorn, 1965, 130 pp.
: Recreational mathematics for the general reader.

Barr, George. *Entertaining with Number Tricks.* McGraw, 1971, 143 pp.

Barr, Stephen. *Mathematical Brain Benders.* Dover, 1982, 224 pp., softbound.
: Includes some puzzles that do not involve mathematics, but there is a good selection of geometry puzzles.

———. *A Miscellany of Puzzles: Mathematical and Otherwise.* Crowell, 1965, 164 pp.

Beiler, Albert H. *Recreations in the Theory of Numbers.* Dover, 1964, 349 pp., paper.
: Covers many topics, including perfect numbers, Mersenne's numbers, amicable numbers, Farey series, and so on.

Benson, William H., and Oswald Jacoby. *Magic Cubes.* Dover, 1981, 142 pp., softbound.
: New methods of construction, with mathematical proofs.

———. *New Recreations with Magic Squares.* Dover, 1976, 195 pp., paper.
: An original work; includes new methods as well as a tabulation of 880 known fourth-order magic squares.

Bergerson, Howard W. *Palindromes and Anagrams.* Dover, 1973, 130 pp., paper.
: Over one thousand anagrams and several hundred palindromes.

Berloquin, Pierre. *100 Numerical Games.* Scribner, 1976, 152 pp.
: Most of these puzzles can be solved only by trial-and-error methods.

Berrondo, Marie. *Mathematical Games.* Prentice, 1983, 211 pp., paper.

Brandes, Louis G. *Math Can Be Fun.* Walch, 1975, 275 pp., paper.
: Games and activities for junior and senior high school students; indexed by topics.

———. *The Math Wizard.* Walch, 1975, 280 pp., paper.

Brooke, Maxey. *Coin Games and Puzzles.* Dover, 1973, 94 pp., paper.
: unabridged republication of the original edition, entitled *Fun for the Money* (Scribner, 1968); contains sixty games and puzzles with many illustrations.

———. *150 Puzzles in Crypt-Arithmetic.* Dover, 1963, 72 pp., paper.

———. *Tricks, Games and Puzzles with Matches.* Dover, 1973, 60 pp., paper.
: 101 puzzles, tricks, and games; 153 illustrations.

Bunch, Bryan H. *Mathematical Fallacies and Paradoxes.* Van Nostrand, 1982, 216 pp.

Carroll, Lewis [C. L. Dodgson]. *Symbolic Logic* and *The Game of Logic.* Two books bound together as *Mathematical Recreations of Lewis Carroll,* vol. 1. 1896. Reprint. Dover, 1958, 199 pp., 69 pp., paper.
: The first book consists of some 400 logic problems involving syllogisms and sorites.

_____. *Pillow Problems* and *A Tangled Tale*. Two books bound together as *Mathematical Recreations of Lewis Carroll*, vol. 2. 1895. Reprint. Dover, 1958, 109 pp., 152 pp., paper.
: Pillow Problems is a classical collection of seventy-two sophisticated brainteasers.

Crypton, Dr. *Timid Virgins Make Dull Company*. Viking, 1984, 192 pp.
: A collection of the author's puzzle columns from *Science Digest* (despite the esoteric title).

Davis, Philip J. *The Lore of Large Numbers*. Random, 1961, 165 pp., cloth and paper.

Dinesman, Howard. *Superior Mathematical Puzzles*. Allen, 1968, 122 pp.

☆ Domoryad, A. P. *Mathematical Games and Pastimes*. Translated from the Russian by Halina Moss. Pergamon, 1964, 298 pp.
: A refreshing approach to "standard" mathematical recreations; well organized; sophisticated and very readable.

Dudeney, H. E. *Amusements in Mathematics*. Dover, 1958, 258 pp., paper.

_____. *The Canterbury Puzzles*. Dover, 1958, 255 pp., paper.
: A distinguished collection of mathematical recreations by a veteran puzzle expert.

_____. *536 Puzzles and Curious Problems*. Edited by Martin Gardner. Scribner, 1967, 428 pp.

☆ Dunn, Angela. *Mathematical Bafflers*. McGraw, 1964, 217 pp.
: Over 150 sophisticated problems involving algebra, geometry, Diophantine equations, probability, logic, and the theory of numbers.

Dunn, Angela Fox. *Second Book of Mathematical Bafflers*. Dover, 1983, 186 pp., softbound.
: Reproductions of 158 problems appearing in Litton Industries' *Problematical Recreations*, Booklets 7–11 inclusive.

Elffers, Joost. *Tangrams, the Ancient Chinese Shapes Game*. Penguin, 1976, 169 pp.
: About 1600 shapes, with solutions; history of tangrams; bibliography.

Emmet, E. R. *Mind-Tickling Brain Teasers*. Emerson, 1978, 255 pp.

_____. *Puzzles for Pleasure*. Emerson, 1972, 310 pp.

Escher, Maurits C. *The Graphic Work of M. C. Escher*. Duell, 1961, 61 pp.
: An unusual and delightful book that has to be seen to be believed; illustrations of tessellations, symmetry groups, and so on, in ornament and design.

☆ Ewing, John, and Czes Kosniowski. *Puzzle It Out: Cubes, Groups, and Puzzles*. Cambridge, 1982, 64 pp., softbound.
: Rubik's Cubes and group theory; excellent illustrations.

Fadiman, Clifton, ed. *Fantasia Mathematica*. Simon, 1958, 298 pp., cloth and paper.

————. *The Mathematical Magpie.* Simon, 1962, 300 pp.
Humorous stories, essays, anecdotes, and rhymes, all related to mathematics.

Friedland, Aaron J. *Puzzles in Math and Logic.* Dover, 1970, 66 pp., paper.
Some one hundred original puzzles of various levels of difficulty, including numbers, geometry, logic, combinations, and probability.

Fujimura, Kobon. *The Tokyo Puzzles.* Edited by Martin Gardner. Scribner, 1978, 184 pp.
An attractive collection of ninety-eight puzzles, some new, many familiar; with solutions.

Gardner, Martin. *Aha! Gotcha: Paradoxes to Puzzle and Delight.* Freeman, 1982, 164 pp., cloth/softbound.
Companion volume to *Aha! Insight;* based on eighty diverse, challenging paradoxes.

————. *Aha! Insight.* Freeman, 1978, 179 pp., softbound.
Sixty-five puzzles, characterized by their "quickie" solutions.

☆ ————. *Mathematical Carnival.* Knopf, 1975, 274 pp.
A worthy successor to the author's six previous books on mathematical games and recreations; the nineteen assorted essays are as fresh as ever.

————. *Mathematical Carnival: A New Round-up of Tantalizers and Puzzles from "Scientific American."* Random, 1977, 274 pp.

————. *Mathematical Circus.* Knopf, 1979, 272 pp.

————. *Mathematical Magic Show.* Knopf, 1977, 284 pp.
A collection of miscellaneous puzzles, many of which are manipulative.

————. *The Numerology of Dr. Matrix.* Simon, 1967, 112 pp.
Unusually stimulating.

————. *Puzzles from Other Worlds.* Random, 1984, 191 pp., softbound.
A sequel to the author's previous book *Science Fiction Puzzle Tales.*

————. *Science Fiction Puzzle Tales.* Potter, 1981, 148 pp., softbound.

————. *The Snark Puzzle Book.* Simon, 1973, 124 pp.
For grade 7 and up.

————. *The Unexpected Hanging and Other Mathematical Diversions.* Simon, 1969, 255 pp.

☆ ————. *Wheels, Life and Other Mathematical Amusements.* Freeman, 1983, 261 pp.
The tenth collection in book form of the author's "Mathematical Games" columns from *Scientific American.*

Gardner, Martin, ed. *Best Mathematical Puzzles of Sam Loyd.* Vol. 1, Dover, 1959, 167 pp., paper; vol. 2, Dover, 1960, 175 pp., paper.
More than a hundred puzzles from Loyd's famous *Cyclopedia of 5,000 Puzzles, Tricks and Conundrums* and a companion volume.

☆ _____. *Martin Gardner's Sixth Book of Mathematical Games from "Scientific American."* Freeman, 1971, 262 pp.; Chicago, 1984, 262 pp.

☆ _____. *New Mathematical Diversions from "Scientific American."* Simon, 1966, 253 pp.; Simon, 1984, 253 pp.
> The third of a series of delightful companion volumes.

☆ _____. *The "Scientific American" Book of Mathematical Puzzles and Diversions.* Simon, 1959, 178 pp., cloth and paper.
> A sophisticated presentation of mathematical recreations.

☆ _____. *The Second "Scientific American" Book of Mathematical Puzzles and Diversions.* Simon, 1961, 253 pp., cloth and paper.
> A companion volume to the above; many new diversions, such as tetraflexagons, Soma cubes, topology, and origami.

☆ Golomb, Solomon W. *Polyominoes.* Scribner, 1965, 182 pp.
> A fascinating study of a modern development in mathematical recreations; a classic.

Graham, L. A., ed. *Ingenious Mathematical Problems and Methods.* Dover, 1959, 237 pp., paper.
> Collection of a hundred sophisticated puzzles contributed by scores of mathematicians to an industrial magazine during an eighteen-year period.

Greenblatt, M. H. *Mathematical Entertainments.* Crowell, 1965; Allen, 1968, 160 pp.

Heath, Royal V. *Mathemagic.* Dover, 1953, 138 pp., paper.
> Number tricks for the parlor magician.

Hoffman, Paul. *Dr. Crypton and His Problems.* St. Martin's, 1983, 192 pp., softbound.

Hollis, Martin. *Tantalizers: A Book of Original Logical Puzzles.* Allen, 1970, 153 pp.

Holt, Michael. *Math Puzzles and Games.* Walker, 1983, 122 pp.

Honsberger, Ross. *Mathematical Morsels.* MAA, 1978, 249 pp.
> A collection of ninety-one miscellaneous sophisticated mathematical problems and recreations; fascinating and brilliantly presented.

Hovanec, Helene. *The Puzzler's Paradise: From the Garden of Eden to the Computer Age.* Paddington, 1978, 160 pp., paper.

Hufford, Roger. *Challenging Puzzles in Logic.* Dover, 1982, 103 pp., softbound.

Hunter, J. A. H. *Challenging Mathematical Teasers.* Dover, 1980, 101 pp., softbound.
> One hundred new problems, somewhat more difficult than those in his earlier books.

_____. *Entertaining Mathematical Teasers.* Dover, 1983, 109 pp., softbound.

_____. *Math Brain Teasers.* Bantam, 1965, 147 pp., paper.

———. *More Fun with Figures.* Dover, 1966, 116 pp., paper.
: A sequel to *Fun with Figures* by the same author.

☆ Hunter, J. A. H., and Joseph S. Madachy. *Mathematical Diversions.* Van Nostrand, 1963; Dover, 1975, 178 pp.

Hurley, James F., ed. *Litton's Problematical Recreations.* Van Nostrand, 1971, 337 pp.
: A compilation of puzzles from the popular Litton Booklets.

Jacoby, Oswald, and William H. Benson. *Mathematics for Pleasure.* McGraw, 1962, 191 pp.

Jargocki, Christopher P. *Science Brain-Twisters, Paradoxes, and Fallacies.* Scribner, 1978, 183 pp.
: Over 160 puzzles based on scientific principles; detailed answers.

Kendall, P. M. H., and G. M. Thomas. *Mathematical Puzzles for the Connoisseur.* Crowell, 1964, 161 pp.
: More than a hundred brainteasers, interestingly presented.

☆ Klarner, David A., ed. *The Mathematical Gardner.* Van Nostrand, 1982, 382 pp.
: Essays on geometry, games, tiling, coding theory, and a wide variety of mathematical recreations.

☆ Konheim, Alan G. *Cryptography: A Primer.* Wiley, 1981, 432 pp.
: Excellent, up-to-date treatment.

☆ Kordemsky, Boris A. *The Moscow Puzzles.* Translated by Abert Perry; edited by Martin Gardner. Scribner, 1982, 309 pp., paper.
: Revised edition of a well-known classic; over three hundred puzzles, many sophisticated.

☆ Kraitchik, Maurice. *Mathematical Recreations.* 2d rev. ed. Dover, 1953, 328 pp.
: A classic; for beginners and experts; chess, bridge, roulette, Russian bank, dominoes, cryptograms, and many other diversions.

Lausmann, Raymond. *Fun with Figures.* McGraw, 1965, 245 pp.
: A collection of more than four hundred problems and puzzles, chiefly involving number sequences and operations, trial-and-error methods, algebraic equations, and Diophantine analysis.

Leeflang, Karel W. H. *Domino Games and Domino Puzzles.* St. Martin's, 1976, 162 pp.
: Comprehensive; emphasizes puzzles rather than games.

Lewis, David B. *Eureka! Math Fun from Many Angles.* Putnam, 1983, 203 pp., paper.

Linn, Charles F. *Puzzles, Patterns, and Pastimes, from the World of Mathematics.* Doubleday, 1969, 136 pp.
: One hundred and eighty-six puzzles, old and new.

Longley-Cook, L.H. *New Math Puzzle Book.* Van Nostrand, 1970, 176 pp.

Lukács, C., and E. Tarjan. *Mathematical Games*. Walker, 1968, 200 pp.

☆ Madachy, Joseph S. *Mathematics on Vacation*. Scribner, 1975, 251 pp.

Mandl, Matthew. *Unusual Mathematical Puzzles, Tricks, and Oddities*. Prentice, 1984, 122 pp.

☆ Matthews, W. H. *Mazes and Labyrinths: Their History and Development*. Dover, 1970, 254 pp., softbound.
> Comprehensive and readable; covers mazes from prehistoric times to early twentieth century.

Maxwell, E. A. *Fallacies in Mathematics*. Cambridge, 1959, 95 pp., cloth and paper.
> Fallacies in geometry, algebra, and calculus, with explanations.

Montroll, John. *Origami for the Enthusiast*. Dover, 1979, 120 pp., softbound.

Moran, Jim. *The Wonders of Magic Squares*. Random, 1982, 227 pp., softbound.

Mott-Smith, Geoffrey. *Mathematical Puzzles for Beginners and Enthusiasts*. 2d rev. ed. Dover, 1954, 248 pp., paper.
> Fine collection of mathematical recreations, well presented.

Northrop, Eugene. *Riddles in Mathematics*. Van Nostrand, 1944, 262 pp.
> Emphasis on mathematical paradoxes and fallacies, including paradoxes of logic, of probability, and of the infinite.

☆ Nourse, James G. *The Simple Solution to Cubic Puzzles*. Bantam, 1981, 64 pp., softbound.
> Suitable for beginners; includes Rubik's Cube and related variations.

☆ O'Beirne, T. H. *Puzzles and Paradoxes*. Oxford, 1965, 238 pp.

Phillips, Dave. *Hidden Treasure Maze Book*. Dover, 1983, 42 pp., softbound.
> Solutions are provided.

Phillips, Hubert [Caliban]. *My Best Puzzles in Logic and Reasoning*. Dover, 1961, 107 pp., paper.
> An excellent collection of logic problems, almost all original.

_____. *My Best Puzzles in Mathematics*. Dover, 1961, 107 pp., paper.

_____. *Problems Omnibus*. 2 vols. Arco, 1960, 1962.
> Some three hundred problems, mostly new.

Rice, Trevor. *Mathematical Games and Puzzles*. St. Martins, 1974, 95 pp.

Rosenberg, Nancy. *How to Enjoy Mathematics with Your Child*. Stein, 1970, 186 pp.
> Figurate numbers, magic squares, intuitive topology, flexagons, paper folding, and so on.

Ruckle, W. H. *Geometric Games and Their Applications*. Pitman, 1983, 187 pp., paper.
> Only calculus and probability are required.

Schaaf, William L. *A Bibliography of Recreational Mathematics.* 4 vols. NCTM, 1970, 148 pp.; 1970, 191 pp.; 1973, 175 pp.; 1978, 172 pp.; paper.
: A classified list of more than 7500 references with many annotations; glossary of nearly 750 technical terms.

☆ Schuh, Fred. *The Master Book of Mathematical Recreations.* Translated by F. Göbrel; edited by T. H. O'Beirne. Dover, 1968, 430 pp., paper.
: A classic; comprehensive and scholarly.

Seymour, Dale G., and Richard Gridley. *Eureka.* Creative Pubs., 1972, 162 pp., softbound.
: Collection of miscellaneous mathematical recreations; not a workbook.

Shepherd, Walter. *Big Book of Mazes and Labyrinths.* Dover, 1973, 112 pp., paper.

☆ Silverman, David L. *Your Move.* McGraw, 1971, 221 pp.
: A collection of tantalizing puzzles based on decision making; most of the 100 problems are accompanied by answers.

Sinkov, Abraham. *Elementary Cryptanalysis: A Mathematical Approach.* New Mathematical Library, no. 22. Singer, 1969, 189 pp.
: Addressed to high school students and nonspecialists.

Smullyan, Raymond. *Alice in Puzzle-Land: A Carollian Tale for Children Under Eighty.* Morrow, 1982, 200 pp.
: More unusual logical puzzles.

———. *The Lady or the Tiger? and Other Logic Puzzles, Including a Mathematical Novel That Features Gödel's Great Discovery.* Knopf, 1982, 226 pp.

☆ ———. *What Is the Name of This Book? The Riddle of Dracula and Other Logical Puzzles.* Prentice, 1978, 241 pp.
: Collection of 200 intriguing logical puzzles.

Snover, Stephen, and Mark Spikell. *Brain Ticklers: Puzzles and Pastimes for Programmable Calculators and Personal Computers.* Prentice, 1981, 162 pp., cloth/softbound.

☆ Steinhaus, Hugo. *Mathematical Snapshots.* Oxford, 1969, 311 pp.
: New edition of a popular collection of mathematical recreations and ideas.

———. *One Hundred Problems in Elementary Mathematics.* Basic, 1963, 174 pp.
: A collection of unusual brain-crackers, most of them brand new.

Straszewicz, Stefan. *Mathematical Problems and Puzzles from the Polish Mathematical Olympiads.* Pergamon, 1965, 367 pp.

Summers, G. J. *Mind Teasers, Logic Puzzles, and Games of Deduction.* Sterling, 1977, 128 pp.

☆ Trigg, Charles W. *Mathematical Quickies.* McGraw, 1967, 210 pp.

Wyler, Rose, and Gerald Ames. *It's All Done with Numbers: Astounding and Confounding Feats of Mathematical Magic.* Doubleday, 1979, 128 pp.

Wylie, C. R., Jr. *101 Puzzles in Thought and Logic.* Dover, 1957, unpaged, paper.
> Not the usual mathematical recreations; instead, puzzles of purely logical nature.

Arithmetic; Numeration; Computation

Adler, Irving. *A New Look at Arithmetic.* Day, 1964, 308 pp.

☆ Asimov, Isaac. *Realm of Numbers.* Houghton, 1959, 200 pp.
> Somewhat unconventional and inviting exposition; exceptionally lucid.

Barlow, Fred. *Mental Prodigies.* Philosophical, 1952, 256 pp.
> Discussion of arithmetical precocity, lightning calculators, chess experts, and so forth.

Bowers, Henry, and Joan Bowers. *Arithmetical Excursions: An Enrichment of Elementary Mathematics.* Dover, 1961, 320 pp., paper.
> Computation; significant figures; averages; number theory; number lore.

☆ Campbell, Howard E. *The Structure of Arithmetic.* Appleton, 1970, 244 pp.
> A text that closely follows the recommendations of the CUPM for the training of elementary school teachers.

Dilson, Jesse. *The Abacus, a Pocket Computer.* St. Martin's, 1968, 1975, 143 pp.

Duncan, Dewey C. *Arithmetic in a Liberal Education.* McGraw, 1969, 495 pp.
> Of interest to readers of all ages.

Dutton, Wilbur H., Colin C. Petrie, and L. J. Adams. *Arithmetic for Teachers.* 2d ed. Prentice, 1970, 315 pp.

☆ Fujii, John N. *Numbers and Arithmetic.* Blaisdell, 1965, 559 pp.

☆ Gechtman, Murray, and James Hardesty. *Arithmetic: Concepts and Skills.* Macmillan, 1968, 272 pp.

Hull, T. E. *Introduction to Computing.* Prentice, 1966, 212 pp.
> An introductory text suitable for freshman or sophomore courses; requires only high school mathematics; numerous exercises.

Japan Chamber of Commerce and Industry. *Soroban, the Japanese Abacus: Its Use and Practice.* Tokyo: Tuttle, 1967, 96 pp., paper.
> An interesting home-study course; includes description of how to construct an abacus.

Kojima, Takashi. *Advanced Abacus: Japanese Theory and Practice.* Tokyo: Tuttle, 1963, 159 pp.

_____. *The Japanese Abacus: Its Use and Theory.* Tuttle, 1954, 102 pp., paper.
   Very clear and complete exposition.

Lay, L. Clark. *The Study of Arithmetic.* Macmillan, 1966, 500 pp.
   Logical approach to the fundamental concepts of arithmetic.

Layton, W. I. *College Arithmetic.* Wiley, 1971, 236 pp.

Ledbetter, David. *Elementary College Arithmetic.* Goodyear, 1969, 266 pp.

Minnick, John H., and Raymond C. Strauss. *Structure of Arithmetic.* Harper, 1966, 528 pp., paper.

☆ Peterson, John A., and Joseph Hashisaki. *Theory of Arithmetic.* Wiley, 1967, 337 pp.

Pullan, J. M. *The History of the Abacus.* Praeger, 1969, 127 pp.
   Well illustrated; extensive bibliography.

☆ Smeltzer, Donald. *Man and Number.* Emerson, 1958, 114 pp.
   Delightfully illuminating.

Sunko, Theodore, and Milton Eulenberg. *Arithmetic: A College Approach.* Wiley, 1966, 225 pp.

Tocquet, Robert. *Magic of Numbers.* Wehman, 1960, 160 pp.
   Mental arithmetic, memory tricks, calculating prodigies, and so on.

Youse, B. K. *Arithmetic: A Modern Approach.* Prentice, 1963, 160 pp.

Algebra; Calculus; Analysis

Adelfio, Salvatore, and Christine Nolan. *Principles and Applications of Boolean Algebra.* Hayden, 1964, 362 pp.

☆ Adler, Irving. *Groups in the New Mathematics.* Day, 1967, 274 pp.

Beckenbach, E. F., and Richard Bellman. *An Introduction to Inequalities.* New Mathematical Library, vol. 3. Random, 1961, 133 pp., paper.

Bowran, A. P. *A Boolean Algebra.* St. Martin's, 1965, 93 pp.

Burton, David A. *An Introduction to Abstract Mathematical Systems.* Addison, 1965, 120 pp.

Byrne, J. Richard. *Number Systems: An Elementary Approach.* McGraw, 1967, 291 pp.

Dean, Richard. *Elements of Abstract Algebra.* Wiley, 1966, 324 pp.
   Emphasis on structural theorems for groups, rings, fields, and vector spaces; for advanced readers.

☆ Dolciani, Mary, et al. *Modern Introductory Analysis.* Houghton, 1964, 651 pp.
   Comprehensive, scholarly material appropriate for precalculus level.

Drobot, Stefan. *Real Numbers.* Prentice, 1964, 102 pp.
   Based on lectures sponsored by NSF for secondary teachers; (1) concept of real numbers; (2) digital representations of real numbers; (3) approximations of real numbers by rationals; (4) cardinality and measures of sets of real numbers.

Drooyan, Irving, Walter H. Hadel, and Frank Fleming. *Elementary Algebra: Structure and Skills.* Wiley, 1966, 358 pp.
   For first-year college and advanced precollege courses.

Dubisch, Roy. *Introduction to Abstract Algebra.* Wiley, 1965, 193 pp.

Dupree, Daniel E., and Frank L. Harmon. *Modern College Algebra.* Prentice, 1965, 250 pp.

Gehr, Merlyn J., and Dale G. Jungst. *Fundamentals of Mathematics: Number Systems and Algebra.* Academic, 1971, 419 pp.

☆ Glicksman, Abraham M., and Harry Ruderman. *Fundamentals for Advanced Mathematics.* Holt, 1964, 651 pp.
   Comprehensive, scholarly material appropriate for precalculus level.

Goodstein, R. L. *Boolean Algebra.* Pergamon, 1963, 140 pp.

Hohn, Franz E. *Applied Boolean Algebra: An Elementary Introduction.* 2d ed. Macmillan, 1966, 139 pp., paper.
   Appropriate for secondary school students.

Kelley, John L. *Algebra: A Modern Introduction.* Van Nostrand, 1965, 335 pp.
   Includes introduction to vector geometry and linear algebra. For advanced readers.

Kilmister, G. W. *Language, Logic, and Mathematics.* English, 1967, 124 pp.

Kleppner, Daniel, and Norman Ramsey. *Quick Calculus.* Wiley, 1965, 294 pp.
   A short manual of self-instruction.

Korovkin, P. P. *Inequalities.* Blaisdell, 1961, 60 pp., paper.

Lankford, Francis, Donald Heikkinen, and Ina Silvey. *Numbers and Operations.* Harcourt, 1970, 461 pp.
   A refresher course for secondary school pupils.

Lockwood, E. H. *A Book of Curves.* Cambridge, 1961, 198 pp.
   Appropriate for self-directed study, for honor students in secondary schools, and for undergraduate college students.

MacDonald, Ina D. *The Theory of Groups.* Oxford, 1968, 254 pp.

McWeeny, Roy. *Symmetry: An Introduction to Group Theory and Its Applications.* Pergamon, 1963, 248 pp.
   Comprehensive and readily understood.

☆ Marjoram, D. T. E. *Exercises in Modern Mathematics*. Pergamon, 1964, 264 pp.
    High school level.

———. *Modern Mathematics in Secondary Schools*. Pergamon, 1964, 266 pp.
    Includes Boolean algebra, groups, matrices, and so on.

☆ Meserve, Bruce E., A. J. Pettofrezzo, and Dorothy Meserve. *Principles of Advanced Mathematics*. Singer, 1964, 758 pp.

☆ Moise, Edwin. *The Number Systems of Elementary Mathematics*. Addison, 1965, 246 pp.

Moore, Charles G. *An Introduction to Continued Fractions*. NCTM, 1964, 95 pp., paper.

Moore, John T. *Elements of Abstract Algebra*. Macmillan, 1962, 203 pp.

Niven, Ivan. *Maxima and Minima without Calculus*. Dolciani Mathematical Expositions No. 6. MAA, 1981, 303 pp., softbound.

☆ ———. *Numbers: Rational and Irrational*. New Mathematical Library, vol. 1. Random, 1961, 136 pp., paper.

North, Roger. *The Art of Algebra: A Simplified Account of Numbers, Equations, Groups, and Continued Fractions*. Pergamon, 1965, 228 pp.
    For the general reader. A reference work that fills the gap between popular expositions and more advanced texts.

O'Brien, Katharine, *Sequences*. Houghton, 1966, 90 pp.
    Supplementary enrichment monograph.

Ohmer, M. M., C. V. Aucoin, and M. J. Cortez. *Elementary Contemporary Algebra*. Blaisdell, 1965, 238 pp.

Olds, C. D. *Continued Fractions*. New Mathematical Library, vol. 9. Random, 1963, 162 pp., paper.

Papy, Georges. *Groups*. St. Martin's, 1964, 220 pp.

☆ Papy, Georges, and Frédérique Papy. *Modern Mathematics*. 2 vols. Macmillan, 1968-69, 459 pp., 435 pp.
    An elementary "foundations" approach regarding mathematics as a set of structures; for mature secondary school pupils.

Parker, Francis D. *The Structure of Number Systems*. Prentice, 1966, 137 pp.

Peressini, Anthony L., and Donald R. Sherbert. *Topics in Modern Mathematics for Teachers*. Holt, 1971, 434 pp.
    Addressed to secondary school teachers; includes theory of numbers, graph theory, Boolean algebra, geometry of complex numbers, set theory, and probability.

Pine, Eli S. *How To Enjoy Calculus*. Arco, 1980, 132 pp.
    Informal introduction to calculus.

Posamentier, Alfred S., and Charles T. Salkind. *Challenging Problems in Algebra; Books I and II.* Macmillan, 1970, 118 pp., 154 pp., paper.

Ribenboim, Paulo. *Functions, Limits, and Continuity.* Wiley, 1964, 140 pp.
Emphasis on understanding concepts rather than calculations.

Roberts, Joseph B. *The Real Number System in an Algebraic Setting.* Freeman, 1962, 145 pp., paper.
For mature readers.

☆ Rueff, M., and M. Jeger. *Sets and Boolean Algebra.* Allen, 1970, 192 pp.
A clear, rigorous, comprehensible treatment of the elements of Boolean algebra; suitable for high school students.

Sawyer, W. W. *A Concrete Approach to Abstract Algebra.* Freeman, 1959, 234 pp., paper.

──────. *What Is Calculus About?* New Mathematical Library, vol. 2. Random, 1961, 118 pp., paper.

Scheid, Francis J. *Elements of Finite Mathematics.* Addison, 1962, 279 pp.
An introductory approach.

Schwartz, Jacob T. *Introduction to Matrices and Vectors.* McGraw, 1961, 163 pp.

Smith, Alton H., and W. A. Albrecht. *Fundamental Concepts of Analysis.* Prentice, 1966, 190 pp.

Snell, K. S., and J. B. Morgan. *Elementary Analysis.* 2 vols. Pergamon, 1966, 240 pp., 220 pp.

Sominskii, I. S. *The Method of Mathematical Induction.* Blaisdell, 1961, 57 pp., paper.

South, G. F. *Boolean Algebra and Its Uses.* Van Nostrand, 1974, 102 pp.
Requires some knowledge of automatic controls for machinery, computer hardware, design of computer systems, and related topics.

Spooner, G. A., and R. L. Mentzer. *Introduction to Number Systems.* Prentice, 1968, 339 pp.

Stanton, Ralph G., and Kenneth D. Fryer. *Topics in Modern Mathematics.* Prentice, 1964, 187 pp.
Based on seminars for secondary school teachers; fields, groups, Boolean algebra, vector spaces, matrices, numerical analysis, probability and statistics, and some types of geometry.

Toeplitz, Otto. *The Calculus, a Genetic Approach.* Chicago, 1963, 192 pp.
A historical introduction to the infinitesimal calculus; for mature readers.

Whitesitt, John E. *Boolean Algebra and Its Applications.* Addison, 1961, 182 pp.
Authoritative; includes many applications to switching circuits and simple games.

☆ Yarnelle, John. *An Introduction to Transfinite Mathematics.* Heath, 1964, 66 pp., paper.
   Informal, authoritative introduction to the fascinating concept of infinity.

Geometry

☆ Adler, Irving. *A New Look at Geometry.* Day, 1966, 416 pp.

Aref, M. N., and William Wernick. *Problems and Solutions in Euclidean Geometry.* Dover, 1968, 258 pp., paper.
   A collection of some 700 challenging "originals"; solutions given for 200 of the problems.

Backman, Carl A., and Robert G. Cromie. *Introduction to Concepts of Geometry.* Prentice, 1971, 320 pp.
   Informal, intuitive treatment.

Ballard, William R. *Geometry.* Saunders, 1970, 249 pp.
   Résumé of plane and solid Euclidean geometry; measurements, coordinate geometry; non-Euclidean geometry, projective geometry; axiomatics; and finite geometries.

Bassetti, F., H. Ruchlis, and D. Malament. *Math Projects: Polyhedral Shapes.* Book-Lab, 1968, 48 pp.

Blumenthal, Leonard M. *A Modern View of Geometry.* Freeman, 1961, 191 pp., paper.
   For the advanced reader. Set theory, postulational systems, affine geometry, projective geometry, metric postulates, and non-Euclidean geometry.

☆ Bold, Benjamin. *Famous Problems of Mathematics: A History of Constructions with Straight Edge and Compasses.* Van Nostrand, 1969, 112 pp.

Bouwsma, Ward D. *Geometry for Teachers.* Macmillan, 1972, 288 pp.
   Intuitive approach; historical illustrations; map-making and other interesting topics.

☆ Bruni, James V. *Experiencing Geometry.* Wadsworth, 1977, 310 pp.
   A beautiful and inspirational book, well illustrated.

Budden, F. J., and C. P. Wormell. *Mathematics through Geometry.* Pergamon, 1964, 230 pp.

☆ Burger, Dionys. *Sphereland: A Fantasy about Curved Spaces and an Expanding Universe.* Crowell, 1965, 205 pp.
   A worthy companion to Abbott's classic *Flatland: A Romance of Many Dimensions.*

Carroll, Lewis. *Euclid and His Modern Rivals.* Dover, 1973, 275 pp., paper.
   Unabridged reprint of an earlier classic.

Choquet, Gustave. *Geometry in a Modern Setting.* Paris: Hermann (U.S. distributor, Houghton), 1969, 142 pp.
   Designed for preservice and in-service secondary school teachers.

Court, N. A. *Modern Pure Geometry for High-School Mathematics Teachers.* Chelsea, 1969, 100 pp.

☆ Coxeter, H. S. M. *An Introduction to Geometry.* Wiley, 1961, 443 pp.

———. *Regular Polytopes.* 3d ed. Dover, 1973, 321 pp., paper.
: First published in 1917; covers polygons, polyhedrons, rotation groups, tessellations, honeycombs, the kaleidoscope, star polyhedrons, higher polytopes, plus new data on shapes in nature as revealed by the electron microscope.

☆ Coxeter, H. S. M., and Samuel Greitzer. *Geometry Revisited.* New Mathematical Library, vol. 19. Random, 1967, 120 pp.

☆ Cundy, H. Martyn, and A. P. Rollett. *Mathematical Models.* Oxford, 1967, 286 pp.

☆ Diggins, Julia E. *String, Straightedge, and Shadow.* Viking, 1965, 160 pp.
: A fresh and dramatic view of the history of geometry in ancient times.

Dorwart, Harold. *The Geometry of Incidence.* Prentice, 1965, 156 pp.

Eaves, J. C., and A. J. Robinson. *Introduction to Euclidean Geometry.* Addison, 1957, 327 pp.

☆ Eccles, Frank M. *An Introduction to Transformational Geometry.* Addison, 1971, 177 pp.
: For high school students as well as prospective secondary school teachers.

Frame, J. S. *Solid Geometry.* McGraw, 1948, 339 pp.
: Not a conventional textbook; original approach to three-dimensional space relations; maps and projections.

Friedrichs, K. O. *From Pythagoras to Einstein.* Random, 1966, 88 pp.

Fujii, John N. *Geometry and Its Methods.* Wiley, 1969, 371 pp.

Ghyka, Matila. *The Geometry of Art and Life.* Dover, 1977, 174 pp., paper.
: A reprint of the original edition; regular polygons and polyhedrons, the golden section, dynamic symmetry, and partitions.

Greenberg, Marvin Jay. *Euclidean and Non-Euclidean Geometries: Development and History.* 2d ed. Freeman, 1980, 400 pp.
: Includes a discussion of geometric transformations and an overview of hyperbolic geometry.

Griffiths, H. B. *Surfaces.* 2d ed. Cambridge, 1981, 128 pp., cloth/softbound.
: Informal but rigorous study of two-dimensional surfaces, the Euler characteristic, etc.

☆ Hemmer, William. *Conceptions of Space: Beginning Geometries for College.* Canfield, 1973, 112 pp.

Hemmerling, Edwin M. *Fundamentals of College Geometry.* Wiley, 1964, 401 pp.

Hilbert, D., and S. Cohn-Vossen. *Geometry and the Imagination.* Chelsea, 1952, 357 pp.

☆ Holden, Alan. *Shapes, Space, and Symmetry.* Columbia, 1971, 200 pp.
Comprehensive and attractive treatment of polyhedrons and polytopes.

Holton, Jean L. *Geometry: A New Way of Looking at Space.* Weybright, 1971, 70 pp.

Hudson, Hilda P. *Ruler and Compass.* Chelsea, 1953.
Reissue: bound with A. B. Kempe, *How to Draw a Straight Line;* E. W. Hobson, *Squaring the Circle;* and others.

☆ Jacobs, Harold R. *Geometry.* Freeman, 1974, 701 pp.
A unique collection of over 1000 drawings, photographs, and cartoons dealing with many aspects of geometry, including inequalities, transformations, constructions, and non-Euclidean geometry.

Jeger, M. *Transformation Geometry.* Allen, 1966, 143 pp.

Johnson, Paul B., and Carol H. Kipps. *Geometry for Teachers.* Brooks, 1970, 262 pp.
Informal geometry.

Kazarinoff, Nicholas D. *Geometric Inequalities.* Random, 1961, 132 pp., paper.

Kespohl, Ruth Carwell. *Geometry Problems My Students Have Written.* NCTM, 1979, 87 pp., paper.

Klein, Felix. *Famous Problems of Elementary Geometry.* Dover, 1956, 92 pp., paper.
Reissue of a well-known classic.

☆ Konkle, Gail S. *Shapes and Perceptions: An Intuitive Approach to Geometry.* Prindle, 1974, 248 pp.

Kostovskii, A. N. *Geometrical Constructions Using Compasses Only.* Blaisdell, 1961, 79 pp., paper.

Krause, Eugene F. *Taxicab Geometry.* Addison, 1975, 88 pp.
Explores a very simple, concrete non-Euclidean geometry and its ramifications.

Levi, Howard. *Foundations of Geometry and Trigonometry.* Prentice, 1960, 347 pp.
Very rigorous, axiomatic approach; for mature readers.

Lines, L. *Solid Geometry.* Macmillan, 1935, 292 pp.; Dover, paper.
Polyhedrons; semiregular and star polyhedrons; crystal forms.

☆ Loomis, Elisha Scott. *The Pythagorean Proposition.* Classics in Mathematics Education series, vol. 1. NCTM, 1968, 284 pp.
Facsimile reproduction of the second edition, 1940; contains 256 proofs.

Lyng, Merwin J. *Dancing Curves.* NCTM, 1978, 16 pp., paper.
Instructions for making a working string model to illustrate conic sections, curves, and surfaces.

Maxwell, E. A. *Deductive Geometry.* Pergamon, 1963, 176 pp., paper.

☆ Meserve, Bruce E. *Fundamental Concepts of Geometry.* Addison, 1955, 321 pp.

Meserve, Bruce E., and Joseph A. Izzo. *Fundamentals of Geometry.* Addison, 1969, 246 pp.

☆ Moise, Edwin. *Elementary Geometry from an Advanced Standpoint.* 2d ed. Addison, 1974, 425 pp.

☆ Niman, John, and Robert Postman. *Mathematics on the Geoboard.* Cuisenaire, 1974, 123 pp.
> In addition to geometric figures, lengths, and areas, deals with probability, number theory, symmetries and structure, and topology.

O'Daffer, Phares G., and Stanley R. Clemens. *Geometry: An Investigative Approach.* Addison, 1976, 445 pp.
> Emphasis is on experiments, activities, and discovery exercises.

Oglivy, C. Stanley. *Excursions in Geometry.* Oxford, 1969, 178 pp.

Ohmer, Merlin M. *Elementary Geometry for Teachers.* Addison, 1969, 152 pp.

Pearce, Peter, and Susan Pearce. *Polyhedra Primer.* Van Nostrand, 1978, 134 pp., paper.
> Nonmathematical treatment; polygons, tessellations, polyhedrons, space filling, and open packings; illustrated; good browsing.

☆ Pedoe, Dan. *Geometry and the Liberal Arts.* St. Martin's (Penguin), 1978, 296 pp., paper.
> A refreshing approach to geometry through the ideas of perspective, proportion, and order; very readable.

Perfect, Hazel. *Topics in Geometry.* Pergamon, 1963, 153 pp., paper.
> Modern geometry, including point transformations, geometry of the triangle, Ptolemy's theorem, Simson's line, projection, inversion, and so on.

Pohl, Victoria. *How to Enrich Geometry Using String Designs.* NCTM, 1986, 68 pp.
> Step-by-step directions, beautifully illustrated, for constructing string designs on polygons and polyhedra. Grades 6–10.

Posamentier, Alfred S., and Charles T. Salkind. *Challenging Problems in Geometry: Books I and II.* Macmillan, 1970, 131 pp., 121 pp., paper.

Posamentier, Alfred S., and William Wernick. *Geometric Constructions.* Walch, 1973, 94 pp., paper.

☆ Prenowitz, Walter, and Meyer Jordan. *Basic Concepts of Geometry.* Blaisdell, 1966, 350 pp.

Rainich, G. Y., and S. M. Dowdy. *Geometry for Teachers.* Wiley, 1968, 228 pp.

Ranucci, Ernest R., and Wilma E. Rollins. *Curiosities of the Cube.* Crowell, 1977, 111 pp.
: Unusual and intriguing.

☆ Reid, Constance. *A Long Way from Euclid.* Crowell, 1963, 292 pp.
: Expository, with accent on historical development.

Ringenberg, Laurence. *College Geometry.* Wiley, 1968, 308 pp.

_____. *Informal Geometry.* Wiley, 1967, 151 pp.
: Uses point-set approach throughout; for teachers of elementary school mathematics.

Rosskopf, M. F., J. L. Levine, and B. R. Vogeli. *Geometry, a Perspective View.* McGraw, 1970, 306 pp.

Shirokov, P. A. *A Sketch of the Fundamentals of Lobachevskian Geometry.* Stechert, 1964, 279 pp.
: An introduction to Lobachevskian geometry intended for a wide range of readers.

Smart, James R. *Introductory Geometry: An Informal Approach.* 2d ed. Brooks, 1972, 317 pp.

Smogorzhevskii, A. S. *The Ruler in Geometrical Constructions.* Blaisdell, 1962, 86 pp., paper.

Sommerville, D. M. Y. *The Elements of Non-Euclidean Geometry.* Dover, 1958, 274 pp., paper.

Stewart, B. M. *Adventures among the Toroids: A Study of Orientable Polyhedra with Regular Faces.* The Author (4494 Wausau Road, Okemos, MI 48863), 1980, 256 pp., softbound.
: A much improved, revised second edition.

Stover, Donald W. *Stereograms.* Houghton, 1966, 44 pp., paper.
: Geometrical drawing, stereoscopic views, and so on.

Stubblefield, Beauregard. *An Intuitive Approach to Elementary Geometry.* Brooks, 1969, 254 pp.
: Appropriate for elementary school teachers.

☆ Tuller, Annita. *A Modern Introduction to Geometries.* Van Nostrand, 1967, 201 pp.

Vasilyov, N. B., and V. L. Gutenmacher. *Straight Lines and Curves.* Import, 1980, 195 pp.
: A delightful and imaginative little book; more than 200 challenging problems in geometry. Experimentation and problem solving.

Weiss, Sol. *Geometry: Content and Strategy for Teachers.* Bogden, 1972, 424 pp.

☆ Wenninger, Magnus J. *Dual Models.* Cambridge, 1983, 156 pp.
: Complement to the author's previous books: *Polyhedron Models* and *Spherical Models.*

☆ _____. *Polyhedron Models.* Cambridge, 1971, 208 pp., paper.

☆ _____. *Spherical Models.* Cambridge, 1979, 145 pp., paper.

☆ Wylie, C. R. *Foundations of Geometry.* McGraw, 1964, 338 pp.

Yaglom, I. M. *Complex Numbers in Geometry.* Academic, 1966. 243 pp., paper.

_____. *Geometric Transformations.* New Mathematical Library, vol. 8. Random, 1962, paper.
: Appropriate for high school students.

_____. *Geometric Transformations III.* Random, 1973, 237 pp.
: Devoted largely to affine and projective transformations.

Yale, Paul B. *Geometry and Symmetry.* Holden, 1968, 288 pp.
: For mature readers; Euclidean, affine, and projective symmetries.

Yates, Robert C. *Curves and Their Properties.* Classics in Mathematics Education series, vol. 4. NCTM, 1975, 245 pp.
: A reprint of the original edition (1952) of a well-known and distinguished reference book.

_____. *The Trisection Problem.* Classics in Mathematics Education series, vol. 3. NCTM, 1971, 68 pp.
: Facsimile reproduction of the 1942 edition; bibliography.

Young, John E., and Grace A. Bush. *Geometry for Elementary Teachers.* Holden, 1971, 273 pp.

Topology; Networks; Polyhedrons

Abbott, Edwin, *Flatland: A Romance of Many Dimensions.* 2d rev. ed. Dover, 1952, 109 pp., paper; Emerson, 1982, 123 pp.
: Reissue of a well-known classic.

Aleksandrov, Pavel S. *Elementary Concepts of Topology.* Dover, 1961, 73 pp., paper.
: An approach off the beaten track.

☆ Arnold, Bradford H. *Intuitive Concepts in Elementary Topology.* Prentice, 1962, 182 pp.
: Bridges the gap between superficial "entertainment" topology and serious, abstract topology.

☆ Barnette, David. *Map Coloring, Polyhedra, and the Four-Color Problem.* MAA, 1983, 168 pp.
: Comprehensive overview of a famous problem, its history, and its ramifications.

☆ Barr, Stephen. *Experiments in Topology.* Crowell, 1964, 210 pp.

Bentley, W. A., and W. J. Humphreys. *Snow Crystals*. Dover, 1931, 227 pp., paper.
  Collection of over 2450 photographs, with an excellent expository introduction.

Berge, Claude. *The Theory of Graphs and Its Applications*. Wiley, 1962, 247 pp.
  A comprehensive treatment of networks and their uses; algebraic topology; for advanced readers.

Bushaw, D. *Elements of General Topology*. Wiley, 1963, 166 pp.

Cameron, A. J. *A Guide to Graphs*. Pergamon, 1970, 158 pp.

☆ Coxeter, H. S. M. *Regular Polytopes*. 2d ed. Macmillan, 1963, 321 pp.
  Polygons and polyhedrons, regular and quasiregular solids, rotation groups, tessellations and honeycombs, the kaleidoscope, star polyhedrons, ordinary polytopes, truncation, Euler's formula, and star polytopes; comprehensive; for advanced readers.

Crown, A. W. *The Language of Triangles*. Vol. 1. Pergamon, 1964, 115 pp.

☆ Cundy, H. Martyn, and A. P. Rollett. *Mathematical Models*. Oxford, 1952, 240 pp.
  Paper folding, dissections, knots, curve stitching, polyhedrons, models, linkages, and machines for drawing curves and for solving equations.

Eckhart, Ludwig. *Four-Dimensional Space*. Translated by A. L. Bigelow and S. M. Slaby. Indiana, 1968, 90 pp.
  Representation of four-dimensional space by means of descriptive geometry (graphics).

Ehrenfeucht, Aniela. *The Cube Made Interesting*. Pergamon, 1964, 83 pp.
  An unusual exposition of the symmetry of the cube, accompanied by helpful anaglyphs.

☆ Fejes Tóth, L. *Regular Figures*. Macmillan, 1964; Pergamon, 1964, 339 pp.
  Comprehensive and rigorous treatment of isometries and plane ornaments; spherical arrangements; hyperbolic tessellations; regular and semiregular polyhderons; regular polytopes; packing and covering problems.

☆ Fujii, John N. *Puzzles and Graphs*. NCTM, 1966, 72 pp., paper.

☆ Gardner, Martin. *The Ambidextrous Universe*. Basic, 1964, 294 pp.
  Entertaining and sophisticated discussion of left-right symmetry and related topics.

Gelfand, I. M., E. G. Glagoleva, and A. Kirillov. *The Method of Coordinates*. MIT, 1967, 69 pp., paper.
  Includes an excellent discussion of four-dimensional space.

Hadwiger, Hugo, and Hans Debrunner. *Combinatorial Geometry in the Plane*. Holt, 1964, 113 pp.
  An intuitive approach to the qualitative aspects of convex bodies.

Henderson, Linda D. *The Fourth Dimension and Non-Euclidean Geometry in Modern Art*. Princeton, 1983, 453 pp., cloth/softbound.

Hilton, Harold. *Mathematical Crystallography and the Theory of Groups of Movements*. Dover, 1963, 262 pp., paper.
> Symmetry; theory of groups; lattices and translations; geometrical operations; infinite groups of movements; regular groups; space partitioning. Advanced and very technical.

☆ Hinton, Charles H. *Speculations on the Fourth Dimension: Selected Writings of C. H. Hinton*. Dover, 1980, 204 pp., softbound.

Jenkins, Gerald, and Anne Wild. *Mathematical Curiosities*. 2 vols. Prentice, 1982, 30 pp. + 30 pp., paper.
> Interesting models of polyhedra, movable flexagons, etc.

Johnson, Donovan A. *Curves in Space*. Exploring Mathematics on Your Own series. McGraw, 1963, 64 pp., paper.

☆ Lindgren, Harry. *Geometric Dissections*. Van Nostrand, 1964, 165 pp.
> Although some puzzles and solutions are included, it is not primarily a book on recreations but rather a systematic treatment.

Manning, Henry P., ed. *The Fourth Dimension Simply Explained*. Dover, 1960, 251 pp., paper.
> Unabridged reprint of first edition (1910) of a well-known collection of popular essays.

Marr, Richard F. *4-Dimensional Geometry*. Houghton, 1970, 41 pp.

☆ Ore, Oystein. *Graphs and Their Uses*. New Mathematical Library, vol. 10. Random, 1963, 131 pp.
> A thoroughly modern approach dealing with mappings, trees, game theory, map coloring, and so on.

Papy, Frédérique, and Georges Papy. *Graph Games*. Crowell, 1971, 33 pp.
> For young readers.

Stover, Donald W. *Mosaics*. Houghton, 1966, 34 pp., paper.
> Polygons, polyhedrons, mosaics; bibliography.

☆ Wenninger, Magnus J. *Polyhedron Models*. Cambridge, 1971, 207 pp.

☆ Weyl, Hermann. *Symmetry*. Princeton, 1952, 168 pp.
> Stimulating; charmingly written.

Theory of Numbers

Barnett, I. A. *Some Ideas about Number Theory.* NCTM, 1961, 80 pp., paper.
Introductory treatment.

☆ Beiler, Albert H. *Recreations in the Theory of Numbers.* Dover, 1964, 349 pp., paper.

Bell, Eric T. *The Last Problem.* Simon, 1961, 308 pp.
A history of Fermat's last problem; for mature readers.

———. *The Magic of Numbers.* McGraw, 1946, 418 pp.

Brown, Stephen I. *Some Prime Comparisons.* NCTM, 1978, 106 pp.
A substantial and thoughtful introduction to the theory of prime numbers.

Davenport, Harold. *The Higher Arithmetic.* Harper, 1960, 172 pp., paper.
An introduction to the theory of numbers; for mature readers.

Friedberg, Richard. *An Adventurer's Guide to Number Theory.* McGraw, 1968, 217 pp.
Historically oriented; brisk, informal style.

Godino, Charles. *Elementary Topics in Number Theory.* Allyn, 1971, 170 pp.

Hoggatt, Verner E., Jr. *Fibonacci and Lucas Numbers.* Houghton, 1969, 92 pp., paper.

Hunter, John. *Number Theory.* Wiley, 1964, 149 pp.

Jones, Burton. *Modular Arithmetic.* Blaisdell, 1964, 91 pp., paper.

LeVeque, William J. *Elementary Theory of Numbers.* Addison, 1962, 132 pp.

☆ Loweke, George P. *The Lore of Prime Numbers.* Vantage, 1982, 259 pp.

☆ Niven, Ivan, and H. S. Zuckerman. *An Introduction to the Theory of Numbers.* 2d ed. Wiley, 1966, 280 pp.

Ogilvy, C. S., and J. T. Anderson. *Excursions in Number Theory.* Oxford, 1966, 167 pp.

Olds, C. D. *Continued Fractions.* New Mathematical Library, vol. 9. Random, 1963, 162 pp., paper.

☆ Ore, Oystein. *Invitation to Number Theory.* New Mathematical Library, vol. 20. Random, 1969, 129 pp., paper.
Delightful; exceptionally lucid style.

Reichmann, W. J. *The Fascination of Numbers.* Oxford, 1957, 176 pp.
A popular exposition of many facets of number theory and related topics.

☆ Reid, Constance. *From Zero to Infinity: What Makes Numbers Interesting*. 3d ed. Apollo, 1961, 161 pp., paper. 3d rev. ed., Crowell, 1965, cloth.
   An unusual and informal approach to the theory of numbers.

Richards, Stephen P. *A Number for Your Thoughts*. The Author (Box 501, New Providence, NJ 07974), 1982, 207 pp., paper.
   Informal introduction to number theory.

Ruderman, Harry. *Mathematical Buds,* Vol. 3. Mu Alpha Theta, 1984, 93 pp., paper.
   Essays on number theory written by talented high school students; for mature readers.

Taylor, L. F. *Numbers*. Faber, 1970, 153 pp.
   Includes discussion of recurring decimals, series, prime numbers, Diophantine equations, finite arithmetic, and Fermat's theorem.

Vorob'iev (or Vorob'ev), N. N. *Fibonacci Numbers*. Blaisdell, 1962, 66 pp., paper; Heath, 1963, paper.

☆ Wisner, Robert J. *A Panorama of Numbers*. Scott, 1970, 176 pp.
   Elementary number theory for fun.

Probability; Statistics

☆ Adler, Irving. *Probability and Statistics for Everyman*. New American, 1966, 256 pp., paper.

Bashaw, W. L. *Mathematics for Statistics*. Wiley, 1969, 350 pp.
   Basic arithmetic and algebra refresher with particular emphasis on inequalities, matrices, vectors, set operations, permutations and combinations, probability, logarithms, and graphs.

Borel, Emile. *Probabilities and Life*. Dover, 1962, 87 pp., paper.

☆ Campbell, Stephen K. *Flaws and Fallacies in Statistical Thinking*. Prentice, 1974, 200 pp.
   Good discussion of the uses and misuses of estimates, graphs, averages, percentages, and probabilities.

Cardano, Girolamo. *The Book on Games of Chance*. Holt, 1961, 57 pp.

Cohen, John, and Mark Hansel. *Risk and Gambling*. Philosophical, 1956, 152 pp.

D'Arcy, J. A. *Chance and Choice*. Thames, 1968, 111 pp.
   For non-mathematics students; probability tree, exponential growth curves, index numbers, game theory, and so forth.

☆ David, F. N. *Games, Gods and Gambling*. Hafner, 1962, 260 pp.
   A history of the theory of probability.

☆ Diamond, Solomon. *The World of Probability: Statistics in Science*. Basic, 1965, 193 pp.
   Appropriate reading for senior high school students.

Dwass, Meyer. *First Steps in Probability*. McGraw, 1967, 282 pp.

Hodges, J. L., and E. L. Lehmann. *Basic Concepts of Probability and Statistics*. Holden, 1970, 450 pp.

Hollander, Myles, and Frank Proschan. *The Statistical Exorcist: Dispelling Statistics Anxiety*. Dekker, 1984, 247 pp.
   Nontechnical; lucid and enjoyable reading.

☆ Hooke, Robert. *How to Tell the Liars from the Statisticians*. Dekker, 1983, 173 pp.
   Comprehensive, stimulating; stresses important statistical concepts.

Huck, Schuyler, and Howard Sandler. *Statistical Illusions: Problems and Solutions*. 2 vols. Harper, 1984, 175 + 174 pp., paper.
   One hundred statistical paradoxes and illusions with complete explanations.

☆ Huff, Darrell, and Irving Geis. *How to Lie with Statistics*. Norton, 1964, 142 pp.
   Ingenious and illuminating.

―――. *How to Take a Chance*. Norton, 1959, 173 pp.
   Humorous commentaries on the vagaries of probability.

Johnson, Donovan A. *Probability and Chance*. Exploring Mathematics on Your Own series. Webster, 1963, 64 pp., paper.

☆ Kimble, Gregory. *How to Use (and Misuse) Statistics*. Prentice, 1978, 290 pp.
   Informal approach to basic statistical concepts.

King, Amy C., and C. B. Read. *Pathways to Probability: History of the Mathematics of Certainty and Chance*. Holt, 1963, 139 pp.

☆ Levinson, Horace. *Chance, Luck and Statistics*. Rev. and enlarged ed. Dover, 1963, 358 pp., paper.
   New edition of a book formerly called *The Science of Chance*; popular introduction for the general reader.

Moskowitz, Martin M. *What Are the Chances? An Introduction to Probability*. Macmillan, 1963, 105 pp.

Mosteller, Frederick, R. E. K. Rourke, and G. B. Thomas. *Probability: A First Course*. Addison, 1961, 319 pp.
   For mature readers.

National Council of Teachers of Mathematics. *Teaching Statistics and Probability*. 1981 Yearbook. NCTM, 1981, 246 pp., hardbound.

☆ Niven, Ivan. *Mathematics of Choice, or How to Count without Counting.* Random, 1965, 202 pp., paper.
> Readable introduction to combinatorial analysis, permutations and combinations, partitions, distributions, probability, configuration problems, and mathematical induction.

Ore, Oystein. *Cardano, the Gambling Scholar.* Princeton, 1953, cloth; Dover, 249 pp., paper; Smith, cloth.

Packel, Edward. *The Mathematics of Games and Gambling.* MAA, 1981, 141 pp., softbound.
> Basic concepts of probability and elementary game theory applied to casino games and social games; nontechnical.

Reichmann, W. J. *Use and Abuse of Statistics.* Oxford, 1962, 336 pp.
> A nonmathematical discussion of statistical methods with emphasis on the design of experiments and the interpretation of statistical data.

Runyon, Richard P. *How Numbers Lie: A Consumer's Guide to the Fine Art of Numerical Deception.* Lewis, 1981, 182 pp., paper.

Slonim, Morris J. *Sampling.* Simon, 1967, 145 pp., paper.
> Nontechnical overview of the field.

☆ Tanur, J., et al., eds. *Statistics: A Guide to the Unknown.* Holden, 1972, 448 pp., cloth and paper.
> A unique, sophisticated exposition.

Thorp, Edward. *Elementary Probability.* Wiley, 1966, 152 pp.
> Requires some knowledge of calculus.

Vesselo, Isaac R. *How to Read Statistics.* Van Nostrand, 1965, 208 pp.
> Descriptive approach to the subject.

Walker, Helen, and Joseph Lev. *Elementary Statistical Methods.* Holt, 1958, 302 pp.

☆ Weaver, Warren. *Lady Luck: The Theory of Probability.* Doubleday, 1963, 392 pp., paper; Dover, 1982, 392 pp., softbound.
> Popular as well as authoritative.

Wolf, Frank L. *Elements of Probability and Statistics.* McGraw, 1974, 450 pp.
> Fairly advanced; basic knowledge of calculus a desirable prerequisite.

Metric Measures

Adler, Peggy, and Irving Adler. *Metric Puzzles.* Watts, 1977, 66 pp.
    For young people; some very easy, some difficult; well written.

Berggren, Don. *The Magnificent Metric System.* Camelot, 1976, 128 pp., paper.

Bitter, Gary, Jerald Mikesell, and Kathryn Maurdeff. *Activities Handbook for Teaching the Metric System.* Allyn, 1976, 370 pp.
    Comprehensive; history, exposition, pupil activity; derived SI units; for elementary and secondary levels; extensive bibliography.

Branley, Franklyn N. *Think Metric!* Crowell, 1972, 53 pp.

Cardwell, Richard. *The Metrics Are Coming! The Metrics are Coming!* Dorrance, 1975, 91 pp.
    Primarily for laymen and for household use.

Cunningham, James B. *Teaching Metrics Simplified.* Prentice, 1976, 184 pp.
    An excellent source book; emphasizes historical backgrounds; good exposition of the nature of measurement.

☆ Deming, Richard. *Metric Power: How and Why We Are Going Metric.* Nelson, 1974, 144 pp.

Donovan, Frank. *Let's Go Metric.* Weybright, 1974, 154 pp.

Hahn, James, and Lynn Hahn. *The Metric System.* Watts, 1975, 63 pp.
    Brief and engaging history of the growth of the metric system, culminating in the SI system; for middle school children.

☆ Hartsuch, Paul J. *Think Metric Now! A Step-by-Step Guide to Understanding and Applying the Metric System.* Penguin, 1974, 120 pp.
    Well written and comprehensive.

Higgins, Jon L., ed. *A Metric Handbook for Teachers.* NCTM, 1974, 137 pp.

☆ Hirsch, S. Carl. *Meter Means Measure: The Story of the Metric System.* Viking, 1973, 126 pp.
    Interesting narrative of the history of the metric system.

Kempf, Albert F., and Thomas J. Richards. *The Metric System Made Simple.* Doubleday, 1977, 150 pp.
    A self-study book suitable for sixth graders and up.

Kurtz, V. Ray. *Metrics for Elementary and Middle Schools.* NEA, 1978, 120 pp.
    Broad in scope; chief emphasis is on mathematics.

Leffin, Walter W. *Going Metric: Guidelines for the Mathematics Teacher, Grades K–8.* NCTM, 1975, 48 pp.

☆ National Bureau of Standards, Special Publication 345. *A Metric America: A Decision Whose Time Has Come.* USGPO, 1971, 170 pp., paper.
   A comprehensive survey; historical background and current activities.

Odom, Jeffrey V., ed. *Successful Experiences in Teaching Metrics.* USGPO, 1976, 115 pp.

O'Niel, P. J. *The Wiley Metric Guide.* Wiley, 1976, 168 pp.

Rahn, Joan Elma. *The Metric System.* Atheneum, 1976, 79 pp.

☆ Ross, Frank, Jr. *The Metric System: Measures for All Mankind.* Phillips, 1974, 132 pp.

Ryan, William T., and Paul Joe Vest. *Modern Metrics Made Easy.* Clearvue, 1976, 78 pp.
   Well organized, nontechnical, and readable; addressed to the general American consumer.

Smart, James R. *Metric Math: The Modernized Metric System—SI.* Brooks, 1975, 92 pp., paper.
   A handy reference book.

Computer Science

General Publications

Ahl, David H., ed. *The Best of Creative Computing*, vol. 1. Creative, 1976, 317 pp.
   General expository survey.

——. *BASIC Computer Games: Microcomputer Edition.* Creative, 1978, 200 pp., paper.

☆ Bernstein, Jeremy. *The Analytical Engine: Computers—Past, Present, and Future.* Random, 1965; Vintage, 1966, 113 pp.
   Historical background; nontechnical introductory exposition of the design, construction, operation, and uses of computers; bibliography.

☆ Bitter, Gary G. *Computers in Today's World.* Wiley, 1984, 437 pp.

Evans, Christopher. *The Making of the Micro: A History of the Computer.* Van Nostrand, 1981, 118 pp.

——. *The Micro Millenium.* Viking, 1980, 320 pp.

Forester, Tom, ed. *The Microelectronics Revolution: The Complete Guide to the New Technology and Its Impact on Society.* MIT, 1981, 589 pp.
   Very comprehensive.

Frates, Jeffrey E., and William Moldrup. *Computers and Life: An Integrative Approach.* Prentice, 1983, 448 pp., paper.

Gallagher, Sharon. *Inside the Personal Computer.* Abbeville, 1984, unpaged.
: An appealing "adult" pop-up book.

Goldberg, Kenneth P., and Robert D. Sherwood. *Microcomputers: A Parents' Guide.* Wiley, 1983, 196 pp., paper.

☆ Goldstine, Herman H. *The Computer from Pascal to von Neumann.* Princeton, 1972, 378 pp.
: Historical emphasis; for mature readers.

Hollerbach, Lew. *A 60-Minute Guide to Microcomputers.* Prentice, 1982, 137 pp., softbound.
: An introductory survey of personal and business computing.

Hopper, Grace M., and Steven L. Mandell. *Understanding Computers.* West, 1984, 490 pp., paper.

Lechner, H. D. *The Computer Chronicles.* Wadsworth, 1984, 391 pp.

McCorduck, P. *Machines Who Think.* Freeman, 1979, 375 pp.
: History of artificial intelligence; emphasis on social approach rather than technical details.

☆ Mowshowitz, Abbe, ed. *Inside Information, Computers in Fiction.* Addison, 1977, 345 pp.
: Emphasis on social issues; extensive bibliography; good indexes.

☆ Noonan, L. *The Age of Computer Literacy.* Oxford, 1983, 334 pp.

Pollack, Seymour, ed. *Studies in Computer Science: MAA Studies in Mathematics.* Vol. 22. MAA, 1984, 408 pp.
: For mature readers.

☆ Raphael, Bertram. *The Thinking Computer: Mind inside Matter.* Freeman, 1976, 322 pp., cloth/paper.
: Broad exposition of computers as general-purpose, symbol-manipulating machines, with some recent applications.

Ritchie, David. *The Binary Brain: Artificial Intelligence in the Age of Electronics.* Little, 1984, 212 pp.

☆ Sanders, Donald H. *Computers Today.* McGraw, 1983, 669 pp.

Schank, Roger C., and Peter G. Childers. *The Cognitive Computer: On Language, Learning, and Artificial Intelligence.* Addison, 1984, 288 pp.

☆ Spencer, Donald D. *Understanding Computers.* Camelot, 1982, 400 pp., paper.
: Fundamentals of computer literacy; emphasis on BASIC.

_____. *The History of Computers.* Camelot, 1979, 224 pp., cloth and paper.

_____. *The Illustrated Computer Dictionary.* Merrill, 1980, 187 pp., paper.
: A useful source book designed for all students of computer science, data processing, and computer literacy in school and college programs.

Squire, Enid. *The Computer, an Everyday Machine.* Addison, 1977, 186 pp.
<blockquote>An excellent, well-rounded treatment.</blockquote>

☆ Weizenbaum, Joseph. *Computer Power and Human Reason: From Judgment to Calculation.* Freeman, 1976, 300 pp.
<blockquote>Thoughtful and perceptive; for mature readers.</blockquote>

Whiteside, Thomas. *Computer Capers: Tales of Electronic Thievery, Embezzlement, and Fraud.* New American, 1978, 166 pp., paper.

Social Impact of Computers

Abshire, Gary M. *The Impact of Computers on Society and Ethics.* Creative, 1980, 120 pp.
<blockquote>Bibliography.</blockquote>

☆ Bolter, J. David. *Turing's Man: Western Culture in the Computer Age.* N. Carolina, 1984, 264 pp.

The Computer: Extension of the Human Mind: Conference Proceedings, July 21–23, 1982. ERIC/CEMREL, 241 pp., paper.

Dorf, Richard C. *Computers and Man.* 3d ed. Boyd, 1982, 560 pp., paper.

Graham, Neill. *The Mind Tool: Computers and Their Impact on Society.* 3d ed. West, 1983, 410 pp., paper.

Holoien, Martin O. *Computers and Their Social Impact.* Wiley, 1977, 264 pp.
<blockquote>Historical background; BASIC language; practical applications; selective chapter bibliographies.</blockquote>

Laver, Murray. *Computers and Social Change.* Cambridge, 1980, 128 pp., paper.

☆ Michie, Donald, and Rory Johnston. *The Knowledge Machine: Artificial Intelligence and the Future of Man.* Morrow, 1985, 192 pp.

☆ Sanders, Donald H. *Computers in Society.* 3d ed. McGraw, 1981, 536 pp.

Smith, H. T., and T. R. G. Green, eds. *Human Interaction with Computers.* Academic, 1980, 369 pp., paper.
<blockquote>Sociological and educational implications.</blockquote>

Stern, Nancy B., and Robert A. Stern. *Computers in Society.* Prentice, 1983, 624 pp., paper.

☆ Turkle, Sherry. *The Computer Culture.* Simon, 1984, 352 pp.

Computers in the Classroom and the Home

☆ Ahl, David. *Computers in Mathematics: A Sourcebook of Ideas.* Creative, 1980, 213 pp.

Albrecht, Bob, Leroy Finkel, and Jerald R. Brown. *BASIC for Home Computers.* Wiley, 1978, 336 pp., paper.
    Programmed for self-instruction; good exposition; quite comprehensive.

Barrette, Pierre, ed. *Microcomputers in K–12 Education: Second Annual Conference Proceedings.* Computer, 1983, 132 pp., paper.

☆ Bitter, Gary G., and Ruth A. Camuse. *Using a Microcomputer in the Classroom.* Reston, 1984, 339 pp., paper.

☆ Bitter, Gary G., and Donna Craighead. *Teaching Computer Literacy.* Sterling Swift, 1984, 317 pp., ring binder.
    Unusual format; interesting "pop ups."

Bitter, Gary G., and Thomas H. Metos. *Exploring with Pocket Calculators.* Simon, 1977, 64 pp.
    A brief history of computing devices together with the uses of a four-function pocket calculator; junior high school level.

☆ Bramble, William J., et al. *Computers in Schools.* McGraw, 1985, 334 pp.

Burt, Bruce C., comp. *Calculators: Readings from the Arithmetic Teacher and the Mathematics Teacher.* NCTM, 1979, 231 pp.

☆ Chambers, Jack A., and Jerry W. Sprecher. *Computer-assisted Instruction; Its Use in the Classroom.* Prentice, 1983, 232 pp.

Doerr, Christine. *Microcomputers and the 3 R's: A Guide for Teachers.* Hayden, 1979, 192 pp., paper.

Dwyer, Thomas, and Margot Critchfield. *BASIC and the Personal Computer.* Addison, 1980, 438 pp., paper.
    Comprehensive; word processing, art, computer graphics, simulation, etc.

☆ Elgarten, Gerald, Alfred Posamentier. *Using Computers.* Addison, 1984, 441 pp.
    Suitable for junior high school level.

☆ Elgarten, Gerald, Alfred Posamentier, and Stephen Moresh. *Using Computers in Mathematics.* Addison, 1983, 574 pp.

☆ Frates, J. *Introduction to the Computer: An Integrated Approach.* Prentice, 1984, 554 pp.

Glicksman, Abraham M. *An Introduction to Linear Programming and the Theory of Games.* Wiley, 1963, 131 pp., paper.
    Excellent exposition, suitable for high school honor programs, college students, teachers, and nonspecialists.

Goldberg, Kenneth P. *Pushbutton Mathematics: Calculator Math Problems, Examples, and Activities.* Prentice, 1982, 197 pp., paper.
    Using calculators in the classroom.

☆ Goldenberg, E. P., et al. *Computers, Education, and Special Needs.* Addison, 1984, 265 pp.

☆ International Business Machines Corporation. *Guide to Learning: Resources for Users of I.B.M. Personal Computers.* I.B.M., 1984, 382 pp.
> A useful resource for those who wish to teach *about* computers, rather than to use computers in the classroom.

Kepner, Henry S., Jr., ed. *Computers in the Classroom.* NEA, 1982, 158 pp., paper.

Lathrop, Ann, and Bobby Goodson. *Courseware in the Classroom.* Addison, 1983, 187 pp., paper.
> Concise, readable; good for beginners.

☆ National Council of Teachers of Mathematics. *Computers in Mathematics Education*, 1984 Yearbook. NCTM, 1984, 244 pp.
> Comprehensive: general issues; computer as a teaching aid; teaching mathematics through programming; diagnostic uses; bibliography.

O'Shea, Tim. *Learning and Teaching with Computers; Artificial Intelligence in Education.* Prentice, 1983, 307 pp.

Papert, Seymour. *Mindstorms: Children, Computers, and Powerful Ideas.* Basic, 1980, 230 pp.
> Education through computers from a Piagetian viewpoint.

☆ Radin, Stephen, and Fayvian Lee. *Computers in the Classroom: A Survival Guide for Teachers.* Science, 1984, 282 pp.
> Excellent source of information for teachers and administrators who wish to introduce computers into their schools.

Rogowski, Stephen J. *Problems for Computer Solution.* Creative, 1980, 181 pp., softbound.

Sloan, Martha E. *Introduction to Minicomputers and Microcomputers.* Addison, 1980, 482 pp.

Spencer, Donald. *The Illustrated Computer Dictionary.* Merrill, 1980, 187 pp., paper.
> A source book for students of computer sciences in schools and colleges.

Tashner, John, ed. *Improving Instruction with Microcomputers: Readings and Resources for Elementary and Secondary Schools.* Oryx, 1984, 272 pp., paper.

Torgerson, Shirley, et al. *Logo in the Classroom.* International, 1984, 201 pp., paper.

☆ Williams, David E. *Mathematics Teacher's Complete Calculator Handbook.* Prentice, 1984, 318 pp., paper.
> Excellent for secondary teachers.

☆ Williams, Brian, and Richard Tingey. *The Urgently Needed Parents' Guide to Computers.* Addison, 1984, 224 pp., paper.

Zehna, Peter W. *Probability by Calculator: Solving Probability Problems with the Programmable Calculator.* Prentice, 1982, 181 pp., paper.

Computer Recreations

☆ Dunlop, David L., and Thomas F. Sigmund. *Problem Solving with the Programmable Calculator: Puzzles, Games, and Simulations with Math and Science Applications.* Prentice, 1983, 227 pp., paper.

☆ Hoffman, Dean, and Lee Mohler. *Mathematical Recreations for the Programmable Calculator.* Hayden, 1982, 322 pp.
Problems for the hand-held calculator.

☆ Kosniowski, Czes. *Fun Mathematics on Your Microcomputer.* Cambridge, 1983, 195 pp., paper.

Nahigian, J. Victor, and William S. Hodges. *Computer Games for Businesses, Schools, and Homes.* Winthrop, 1979, 157 pp., paper.
Twenty-seven computer games written in BASIC; includes tic-tac-toe, Russian roulette, poker, tennis, and basketball.

☆ Råde, Lennart, and Burt A. Kaufman. *Adventures with Your Hand Calculator.* CEMREL, 1977, 131 pp., paper.
Interesting challenges for bright students; problems dealing with magic squares, palindromes, permutations, and so on.

Reid-Green, Keith. *Games Computers Play.* Digital, 1984, 242 pp., softbound.
Includes outer space, ballistic trajectories, race tracks, mazes, artificial intelligence.

Rogers, James T. *The Calculating Book: Fun and Games with your Pocket Calculator.* Random, 1975, 81 pp.
Brief discussion of the operation of a medium-priced pocket calculator followed by about a hundred exercises, games, tricks, and cartoons.

Rogowski, Stephen J. *Computers for Sea and Sky.* Creative, 1982, 105 pp., paper.
Interesting applications: sailing, surveying, navigation, meteorology, astronomy, etc.

Schlossberg, Edwin, and John Brockman. *The Pocket Calculator Game Book.* Morrow, 1975, 158 pp., paper.
Presents fifty games and puzzles for one or more players; requires only the simplest of calculators.

Spencer, Donald D. *Fun with Computers and BASIC.* Camelot, 1977, 96 pp., paper.
Partial list of BASIC programs includes prime numbers, Fibonacci numbers, Pythagorean triples, perfect numbers, and Pascal's triangle.

☆ ———. *Game Playing with Computers.* Camelot, 1975, 456 pp.
Presents over seventy games, puzzles, and mathematical recreations; also outlines twenty-five game-playing programs in FORTRAN and BASIC.

Professional Books for Teachers

Mathematical Education; Trends; Curriculum; Adminstration

Aichele, Douglas B., ed. *Mathematics Teacher Education: Critical Issues and Trends.* NEA, 1978, 64 pp., cloth and paper.

Association of Teachers of Mathematics [Great Britain]. *Mathematical Reflections: Contributions to Mathematical Thought and Teaching.* Cambridge, 1970, 250 pp.
> Contains eighteen articles by leaders in British mathematical education; geometry is the unifying theme.

☆ Begle, E. G. *Critical Variables in Mathematics Education: Findings from a Survey of the Empirical Literature.* NCTM, 1979, 165 pp.
> A basic reference source for researchers in mathematics education.

☆ Bidwell, James K., and Robert G. Clason. *Readings in the History of Mathematics Education.* NCTM, 1970, 706 pp.

Commission on the Education of Teachers of Mathematics. *Guidelines for the Preparation of Teachers of Mathematics.* NCTM, 1981, 21 pp.

Committee on the Undergraduate Program in Mathematics. *Recommendations for a General Mathematical Sciences Program.* MAA, 1981, 102 pp., softbound.

Félix, Lucienne. *Modern Mathematics and the Teacher.* Cambridge, 1966, 128 pp.

Freudenthal, Hans. *Mathematics as an Educational Task.* Reidel, 1972, 684 pp., cloth and paper.
> Thoughtful and comprehensive; places mathematical education in the context of general education.

Gage, N. L. *The Scientific Basis of the Art of Teaching.* Teachers, 1978, 122 pp., paper.

☆ Griffiths, H. B., and A. G. Howson. *Mathematics: Society and Curricula.* Cambridge, 1974, 423 pp.
> Comprehensive and scholarly; emphasis on British practice; explores the nature of mathematics as well as the impact of the cultural environment.

Henderson, George L. *Mathematics Supervisor's Handbook.* Merrill, 1971, 151 pp.

Howson, A. G., ed. *Developments in Mathematical Education: Proceedings of the Second International Congress on Mathematical Education.* Cambridge, 1973, 318 pp.

Howson, Geoffrey. *A History of Mathematics Education in England.* Cambridge, 1982, 294 pp.
>From Robert Recorde to the present.

☆ International Commission of Mathematical Instruction. *New Trends in Mathematics Teaching.* Vol. 4. Unipub, 1979, 285 pp., paper.

Jacobs, Harold. R. *Mathematics: A Human Endeavor: A Book for Those Who Think They Don't Like the Subject.* 2d ed. Freeman, 1982, 649 pp.
An improved and expanded revision of a best seller.

Kapur, J. N., ed. *Thoughts on Mathematical Education.* Ram, 1973, 136 pp.
A collection of observations made by 150 mathematicians and mathematics educators.

Kemeny, John G. *Random Essays on Mathematics, Education and Computers.* Prentice, 1964, 163 pp.
Of interest to students, teachers, and administrators on the secondary school and college levels.

Kidd, Kenneth P., Shirley S. Myers, and David M. Cilley. *The Laboratory Approach to Mathematics.* SRA, 1970, 282 pp.

☆ Kline, Morris. *Why Johnny Can't Add: The Failure of the New Math.* St. Martin's, 1973, 173 pp., paper.
A critical but thoughtful and challenging appraisal.

☆ ———. *Why the Professor Can't Teach.* St. Martin's, 1977, 288 pp.
A thought-provoking discussion with implications for mathematics at both elementary and secondary school levels.

Lockard, J. David, ed. *Seventh Report of the International Clearinghouse on Science and Mathematics Curricular Developments.* Clearinghouse, 1970, 695 pp.

Lovett, C. James, and Ted Snyder, eds. *Resources for Teaching Mathematics in Bilingual Classrooms.* ERIC, 1979, 56 pp.

MAA Committee on Advisement and Personnel. *Professional Opportunities in the Mathematical Sciences.* 10th ed. MAA, 1978, 35 pp., paper.
Employment opportunities for mathematically trained individuals: industrial, governmental, statistical, research, insurance, and teaching.

McIntosh, Jerry A., ed. *Perspectives on Secondary Mathematics Education.* Prentice, 1971, 259 pp., paper.
A collection of appropriate readings in comtemporary secondary school mathematics; for prospective teachers.

Morris, Robert, ed. *Studies in Mathematics Education.* 2 vols. Unipub, 1980, 1981, 131 pp. + 179 pp., paper.

National Council of Teachers of Mathematics. *Evaluation in Mathematics.* Twenty-sixth Yearbook. NCTM, 1961, 216 pp.

———. *A History of Mathematics Education in the United States and Canada.* Edited by Phillip S. Jones. Thirty-second Yearbook. NCTM, 1970, 557 pp.

☆ ———. *Research in Mathematics Education.* Edited by Richard J. Shumway. NCTM, 1980, 487 pp.
   A comprehensive, definitive source book in its field.

☆ ———. *Secondary School Mathematics Curriculum.* 1985 Yearbook. NCTM, 1985, 250 pp.
   A timely, in-depth discussion.

Poirot, James L. *Computers and Education.* Sterling Swift, 1980, 96 pp., paper.
   General overview of the status of the computer in education today; somewhat superficial, but a helpful bibliography.

Postlethwaite, T. Neville. *School Organization and Student Achievement.* [UNESCO Institute for Education.] Wiley, 1968, 146 pp.
   A study based on achievement in mathematics in twelve countries.

Prime-80: Proceedings of a Conference on Prospects in Mathematics Education in the 1980's. MAA, 1979, 84 pp., paper.
   Emphasizes the importance of students' precollege preparation in mathematics.

Research and Development in Education: Mathematics. Proceedings of a National Conference on Needed Research in Education. 1968, 142 pp. Can be ordered from NCTM.

School Mathematics Study Group and Survey of Recent East European Mathematical Literature. *Soviet Studies in the Psychology of Learning and Teaching Mathematics.* 14 vols. NCTM, 1969–1975, paper.

Servais, W., and T. Varga, eds. *Teaching School Mathematics.* Penguin, 1971, 308 pp., paper.
   For advanced students of mathematics education; a UNESCO publication that stresses the European point of view.

Skolnick, Joan, Carol Langbort, and Lucille Day. *How to Encourage Girls in Math and Science.* Prentice, 1982, 192 pp., softbound.
   A courageous approach to a timely problem.

Steen, Lynn Arthur. *Undergraduate Mathematics Education in the People's Republic of China.* Report of a 1983 American Delegation. MAA, 1984, 99 pp., paper.

☆ Steen, Lynn Arthur, and Donald J. Albers. *Teaching Teachers, Teaching Students: Reflections on Mathematical Education.* Birkhauser, 1981, 136 pp.
   Report on the Fourth International Congress of Mathematical Education.

Suydam, Marilyn N., and Alan Osborne. *The Status of Pre-College Science, Mathematics, and Social Science Education: 1955-1975.* Mathematics Education, vol. 2. SMEAC, 1977, 292 pp., paper.

Swetz, Frank. *Mathematics Education in China: Its Growth and Development.* MIT, 1974, 364 pp.
> Teacher education; curriculum; examinations; pedagogy; textbooks; and so on. Impact of social-political factors with emphasis on events of the last quarter-century; bibliography.

Swetz, Frank J. *Socialist Mathematics Education.* Burgundy, 1978, 421 pp., cloth and paper.

☆ United Nations Educational, Scientific, and Cultural Organization. *New Trends in Mathematics Teaching.* UNESCO, 1973, 145 pp.

Vesselo, I. R., ed. *The Further Training of Mathematics Teachers at the Secondary Level.* International Studies in Education, no. 22. Hamburg: UNESCO Institute for Education, 1969, 90 pp.
> Report on international meeting on teacher training in various countries.

☆ Vogeli, Bruce. *Soviet Secondary Schools for the Mathematically Talented.* NCTM, 1968, 100 pp., paper.

☆ Wheeler, Roger F. *Rethinking Mathematical Concepts.* Halsted, 1981, 314 pp.
> Scholarly; suggested professional reading for teachers.

Psychology of Learning Mathematics

Akst, Geoffrey. *Improving Mathematical Skill.* Jossey, 1981, 138 pp., paper.

Bartkovich, Keven G., and William C. George. *Teaching the Gifted and Talented in the Mathematics Classroom.* NEA, 1980, 48 pp., paper.
> Discusses the identification of mathematically gifted students and gives suggestions for following through; brief but practical.

Bransford, John, and Barry Stein. *The IDEAL Problem Solver: A Guide for Improving Thinking, Learning, and Creativity.* Freeman, 1984, 150 pp., paper.
> A practical approach.

Brush, Lorelei R. *Encouraging Girls in Mathematics: The Problem and the Solution.* Abt, 1980, 176 pp.
> A sober, thought-provoking, and extensive discussion; excellent bibliography.

Chapman, L. R., ed. *The Process of Learning Mathematics.* Pergamon, 1972, 392 pp.

☆ Copeland, Richard W. *How Children Learn Mathematics: Teaching Implications of Piaget's Research.* 2d ed. Macmillan, 1974, 374 pp.

☆ Davis, Robert B. *Learning Mathematics: The Cognitive Science Approach to Mathematics Education.* Ablex, 1984, 392 pp.
> An attempt to bridge the gap between the researcher and the classroom teacher.

Dienes, Z. P. *An Experimental Study of Mathematics Learning.* Humanities, 1963, 207 pp.

———. *The Power of Mathematics.* Humanities, 1964, 176 pp.

Dienes, Z. P., and E. W. Golding. *Learning Logic, Logical Games.* Herder, 1966, 80 pp., paper.

☆ Dienes, Z. P., and M. A. Jeeves. *Thinking in Structures.* Hutchinson, 1965, 128 pp.

Emmet, E. R. *Learning to Think.* Emerson, 1980, 173 pp.
Of special interest to mathematics teachers.

Fey, James T. *Patterns of Verbal Communication in Mathematics Classes.* Teachers, 1970, 92 pp.

Fischbein, E., ed. *The Intuitive Sources of Probabilistic Thinking in Children.* Reidel, 1975, 204 pp.

Flanagan, John C., Robert F. Mager, and William M. Shanner. *Mathematics Behavioral Objectives: A Guide to Individualizing Learning.* Westinghouse, 1971, 138 pp.

Fuson, Karen C., and William E. Geeslin, eds. *Explorations in the Modeling of the Learning of Mathematics.* SMEAC, 1979, 235 pp.

Hademos, James G. *Piagetian Handbook for Teachers.* The Author (Angelo State University, San Angelo, TX 76901), 1975.

Hawley, Robert C., and Isabel L. Hawley. *Building Motivation in the Classroom: A Structured Approach to Improving Student Achievement.* ERA, 1979, 108 pp.

☆ Higgins, Jon L. *Mathematics Teaching and Learning.* Jones, 1973, 228 pp.
Theory and practice; good analyses of the principal learning theories.

☆ Hilton, Peter, and Jean Pedersen. *Fear No More: An Adult Approach to Mathematics.* Addison, 1983, 281 pp.
For mature readers; a book for independent study.

Holt, Michael, and Zoltan Dienes. *Let's Play Math.* Walker, 1973, 184 pp.
Emphasis on child psychology, the use of games, and activities to get children to *do* mathematics.

Kamii, Constance, and Rheta DeVries. *Piaget, Children, and Number.* NCTM, 1976, 52 pp.

Kaye, Barrington. *Participation in Learning: A Progress Report on Some Experiments in the Training of Teachers.* Allen, 1970, 239 pp.

Keating, Daniel P., ed. *Intellectual Talent: Research and Development.* Hopkins, 1976, 346 pp.
A sequel to *Mathematical Talent: Discovery, Description, and Development* by Stanley, Keating, and Fox (Hopkins, 1974). Of interest to supervisors, guidance counselors, and researchers.

Kilpatrick, Jeremy, Izaak Wirszup, Edward Begle, and James Wilson, eds. *Soviet Studies in the Psychology of Learning and Teaching Mathematics.* Vols. 1–14. NCTM, 1969–1975.
<blockquote>Fourteen volumes published by the University of Chicago during the period 1969 to 1975.</blockquote>

Kogelman, Stanley, and Joseph Warren. *Mind over Math.* Dial, 1978, 239 pp.
<blockquote>An examination of the negative feelings about mathematics that some people have; emphasizes the emotional factors involved.</blockquote>

Lee, Doris M. *A Background to Mathematical Development.* Oldbourne, 1962, 227 pp. Order from British Book Service.
<blockquote>Psychology-of-learning approach.</blockquote>

☆ Lichtenberg, Betty K., and Andria P. Troutman, eds. *Fostering Creativity through Mathematics.* FCTM, 1974, 142 pp.
<blockquote>Excellent for the professional library.</blockquote>

Lovell, Kenneth. *The Growth of Basic Mathematical and Scientific Concepts in Children.* London, 1961, 154 pp.
<blockquote>Leans heavily on the work of Piaget, Inhelder, and the Geneva school.</blockquote>

National Council of Teachers of Mathematics. *The Learning of Mathematics.* Twenty-first Yearbook. NCTM, 1953, 364 pp.

――――. *The Mathematical Education of Exceptional Children and Youth: An Interdisciplinary Approach,* edited by Vincent J. Glennon. NCTM, 1981, 408 pp.

――――. *The Slow Learner in Mathematics.* Thirty-fifth Yearbook. NCTM, 1972, 528 pp.

Piaget, Jean. *The Child's Conception of Number.* Humanities, 1952, 248 pp., cloth; Norton, 1965, paper.

Piaget, Jean, and Bârbel Inhelder. *The Child's Conception of Space.* Humanities, 1948, 512 pp.

――――. *The Origin of the Idea of Chance in Children.* Translated by Lowell Leake, Jr., Paul Burrell, and Harold Fishbein. Norton, 1975, 251 pp.
<blockquote>A significant addition to Piaget's work.</blockquote>

Piaget, Jean, Bârbel Inhelder, and Alina Szeminska. *The Child's Conception of Geometry.* Basic, 1960, 411 pp., cloth; Harper, paper.

Rosskopf, Myron F. *Children's Mathematical Concepts: Six Piagetian Studies in Mathematics Education.* Teachers, 1975, 214 pp.

☆ Rosskopf, Myron F., Leslie P. Steffe, and Stanley Taback, eds. *Piagetian Cognitive-Development Research and Mathematical Education.* A conference report. NCTM, 1971, 243 pp.

☆ Scandura, Joseph M. *Problem Solving.* Academic, 1977, 591 pp.
<blockquote>An excellent and scholarly treatment; comprehensive; based on research.</blockquote>

Skemp, Richard R. *The Psychology of Learning Mathematics*. Pelican, Penguin, 1972, 255 pp., paper.

☆ Stanley, Julian C., Daniel P. Keating, and Lynn H. Fox, eds. *Mathematical Talent: Discovery, Description, and Development*. Hopkins, 1974, 215 pp., cloth and paper.
> A scholarly discussion of mathematical and scientific precocity; based on a five-year study of talented junior high school students; nine independent essays by qualified psychologists.

Steffe, Leslie P., ed. *Research on Mathematical Thinking of Young Children: Six Empirical Studies*. NCTM, 1975, 202 pp.
> Summarizes the findings of these studies and compares them with the results of other similar research; very evocative monograph.

Tobias, Sheila. *Overcoming Math Anxiety*. Norton, 1978, 278 pp.
> An examination of the causes of anxiety about mathematics, particularly among women.

Wertheimer, Max. *Productive Thinking*. Harper, 1959, 320 pp.
> Penetrating analysis of thought processes in mathematics; chapter on the area of a parallelogram is a classic; chapter on the sum of the angles of a polygon is brilliant.

Whimbey, Arthur, and Jack Lochhead. *Problem Solving and Comprehension: A Short Course in Analytic Reasoning*. 3d ed. Franklin, 1982, 343 pp., softbound.

Problem-solving Techniques

Averbach, Bonnie, and Orin Chein. *Mathematics: Problem Solving through Recreational Mathematics*. Freeman, 1981, 400 pp.

Brousseau, Bro. Alfred. *Saint Mary's College Mathematics Contest Problems*. Creative Pubs., 1972, 114 pp., softbound.
> For junior and senior high schools; over 400 problems with solutions; a useful source book.

☆ Brown, Stephen I., and Marion I. Walter. *The Art of Problem Posing*. Franklin, 1983, 147 pp., softbound.
> Excellent; examples from high school mathematics show how problem solving is related to problem posing.

Burkhart, Hugh, ed. *Mathematics Education Information Report: An International Review of Applications in School Mathematics—the Elusive El Dorado*. ERIC, 1983, 159 pp., paper.
> Special emphasis on problem solving.

Dunlop, David L., and Thomas F. Sigmund. *Problem Solving with the Programmable Calculator: Puzzles, Games and Simulations with Math and Science Applications*. Prentice, 1983, 227 pp., paper.

Greenes, Carole E., Rika Spungin, and Justine M. Dombrowski. *Problem-Mathics: Mathematical Challenge Problems with Solution Strategies*. Creative Pubs., 1977, 141 pp., softbound.
> A workbook of mathematical recreations.

Harvey, John G., and Thomas A. Romberg, eds. *Problem-Solving Studies in Mathematics.* Wisconsin, 1980, 287 pp., paper.

Horn, Carin E., and James L. Poirot. *Computer Literacy: Problem Solving with Computers.* Sterling Swift, 1981, 304 pp., paper.

Kelman, Peter, et al. *Computers in Teaching Mathematics.* Addison, 1983, 308 pp., softbound.
> Emphasizes use of computers for instruction in problem solving.

☆ Krulik, Stephen, and Jesse A. Rudnick. *Problem Solving: A Handbook for Teachers.* Allyn, 1980, 227 pp., paper.

☆ Larson, Loren C. *Problem Solving through Problems.* Springer, 1983, 332 pp.
> A comprehensive anthology of problems; a useful guide for instructors.

☆ Lester, Frank K., and Joe Garofalo, eds. *Mathematical Problem Solving: Issues in Research.* Franklin, 1982, 139 pp., paper.
> Comprehensive; bibliography.

Meyer, Carol, and Tom Sallee. *Make It Simpler: A Practical Guide to Problem Solving in Mathematics.* Addison, 1983, 282 pp., 8½" × 11", softbound.

Moses, Stanley. *The Art of Problem Solving.* Transworld, 1974, 183 pp.

☆ Polya, George. *Mathematical Discovery: On Understanding Learning, and Teaching Problem Solving,* Combined edition. Wiley, 1981, 220 pp., paper.

Schoenfeld, Alan. *Problem Solving in the Mathematics Curriculum.* MAA, 1983, 137 pp., 8½" × 11", softbound.

Snover, Stephen, and Mark Spikell. *Mathematical Problem Solving with the Microcomputer.* Prentice, 1982, 190 pp., softbound.

Whimbey, Arthur, and Jack Lochhead. *Problem Solving and Comprehension.* 3d ed. Franklin, 1982, 343 pp., softbound.
> Comprehensive and analytical; a practical approach.

Yeshurun, Shraga. *The Cognitive Method: A Strategy for Teaching Word Problems.* NCTM, 1979, 50 pp.

Teaching Secondary School Mathematics

☆ Aichele, Douglas B., and Robert E. Reys, eds. *Readings in Secondary School Mathematics.* Prindle, 1977, 582 pp., paper.
> Over fifty articles and excerpts dealing with the teaching of secondary school mathematics; a valuable resource; bibliography.

Bartkovich, K. G., and W. C. George. *Teaching the Gifted and Talented in the Mathematics Classroom.* NEA, 1980, 48 pp., paper.

Bassler, Otto C., and John R. Kolb. *Learning to Teach Secondary School Mathematics*. International, 1971, 434 pp.

Bell, Frederick H. *Teaching and Learning Mathematics (in Secondary Schools)*. Brown, 1978, 562 pp.

Brissenden, T. H. F. *Mathematics Teaching: Theory and Practice*. Harper, 1980, 177 pp., cloth/paper.

☆ Butler, Charles H., F. Lynwood Wren, and J. Houston Banks. *The Teaching of Secondary Mathematics*. 5th ed. McGraw, 1970, 597 pp.
  Revision of a well-known work.

Collier, C. Patrick. *Geometry for Teachers*. Houghton, 1976, 331 pp.

Cooney, Thomas J., Edward J. Davis, and K. B. Henderson. *Dynamics of Teaching Secondary School Mathematics*. Houghton, 1975, 448 pp.

☆ Dienes, Z. P., and E. W. Golding. *Approach to Modern Mathematics*. Herder, 1971, 173 pp.
  A discussion, based on research, of learning and teaching mathematics.

Fawcett, Harold P., and Kenneth Cummins. *The Teaching of Geometry from Counting to Calculus*. Merrill, 1970, 437 pp.

☆ Fletcher, T. J., ed. *Some Lessons in Mathematics: A Handbook on the Teaching of "Modern" Mathematics*. Cambridge, 1964, 363 pp., paper.
  An unusual and timely book. Topics discussed include binary arithmetic; sets and relations; movement geometry; vectors and matrices; and numerical methods.

Fremont, Herbert. *Teaching Secondary Mathematics through Applications*. 2d ed. Prindle, 1979, 342 pp.

Gattegno, Caleb. *The Common Sense of Teaching Mathematics*. Educational, 1974, 144 pp.
  Rather theoretical and somewhat unorthodox, but stimulating.

Good, Thomas L. *Active Mathematics Teaching*. Longmans, 1983, 246 pp.

Hollingshead, Irving. *Field Applications of Mathematics*. Berks, 1980, 128 pp., paper.
  A reference work covering navigation, cartography, and contour mapping as well as surveying; slightly technical but well written; eleventh-grade level.

Hoover, Kenneth H. *The Professional Teacher's Handbook: A Guide for Improving Instruction in Today's Middle and Secondary Schools*. 2d ed. Allyn, 1976, 184 pp., paper.

Howes, Virgil M., ed. *Individualizing Instruction in Science and Mathematics: Selected Readings on Programs, Practices, and Uses of Technology*. Macmillan, 1970, 192 pp.

☆ Johnson, Donovan A., and Gerald R. Rising. *Guidelines for Teaching Mathematics*. 2d ed. Wadsworth, 1972, 544 pp.

Kepner, Henry S., Jr., and David R. Johnson. *Guidelines for the Tutor of Mathematics*. NCTM, 1977, 28 pp.

☆ Krulik, Stephen, and Ingrid B. Weise. *Teaching Secondary School Mathematics*. Saunders, 1975, 243 pp.
> Brief, but very cogent; particular emphasis on methodology and strategy; a practical guide.

Leonard, William A. *No Upper Limit: The Challenge of the Teacher of Secondary Mathematics*. Creative Tchg., 1977, 122 pp.
> A collection of problems, anecdotes, and classroom experiences; many suggestions for teaching strategies.

☆ Marjoram, D. T. E. *Modern Mathematics in Secondary Schools*. Pergamon, 1964, 266 pp.
> Professionalized subject matter. Includes set theory, Boolean algebra, groups, matrices, vectors, inequalities, linear programming, statistics, and methods of teaching these topics.

McIntosh, Jerry, ed. *Perspectives on Secondary Mathematics Education*. Prentice, 1971, 259 pp.

Morine, Harold, and Greta Morine. *Discovery: A Challenge to Teachers*. Prentice, 1973, 242 pp., paper.
> Emphasis on discovery methods and individual responsibility of the pupil.

National Council of Teachers of Mathematics. *Developing Computational Skills*. 1978 Yearbook. NCTM, 1978, 256 pp.

————. *Organizing for Mathematics Instruction*. 1977 Yearbook. NCTM, 1977, 256 pp.

Nowlan, Robert A., and Robert M. Washburn. *Geometry for Teachers*. Harper, 1975, 391 pp.

Osborne, Alan, ed. *An In-Service Handbook for Mathematics Education*. NCTM, 1977, 260 pp.

☆ Posamentier, Alfred S. *Teaching Secondary School Mathematics*. Merrill, 1981, 408 pp., paper.
> Good overview: excellent for enrichment topics.

Scopes, P. G. *Mathematics in Secondary Schools—a Teaching Approach*. Cambridge, 1973, 179 pp.

Thwaites, Bryan. *On Teaching Mathematics*. Pergamon, 1961, 116 pp., paper.

Travers, Kenneth J. *012345678910 Mathematics Teaching*. Harper, 1977, 591 pp.
> A general text on the methods of teaching mathematics, but omits a discussion of observation and practice teaching.

☆ Willoughby, Stephen S. *Contemporary Teaching of Secondary School Mathematics*. Wiley, 1967, 430 pp.

Activities; Projects; Enrichment; Contests; Visual Aids

Artino, Ralph, Anthony Gaglione, and Niel Shell. *The Contest Problem Book IV.* MAA, 1982, 184 pp., softbound.
>Contains the Annual High School Mathematics Examinations given from 1973 through 1982, with solutions.

Baur, Gregory R., and Linda Olsen George. *Helping Children Learn Mathematics: A Competency-based Laboratory Approach.* Cummings, 1976, 406 pp.
>Emphasis on objectives and lesson plans.

Bezuszka, Stanley, Margaret Kenney, and Linda Silvey. *Designs from Mathematical Patterns.* Creative Pubs., 1978, 202 pp., softbound.
>An activity workbook; includes use of modular arithmetic, magic squares, Fibonacci numbers; bibliography, 27 references.

———. *Tessellations: The Geometry of Patterns.* Creative Pubs., 1977, 169 pp., softbound.
>Essentially a consumable workbook; extensive bibliography, 54 references.

Bitter, Gary G., and Jerald L. Mikesell. *Activities Handbook for Teaching with the Hand-held Calculator.* Allyn, 1980, 312 pp., paper.

Bitter, Gary G., Jerald L. Mikesell, and Kathryn Maurdeff. *Activities Handbook for Teaching the Metric System.* Allyn, 1976, 378 pp.

Bolt, Brian. *Mathematical Activities: A Resource Book for Teachers.* Cambridge, 1982, 207 pp., paper.
>Grades 7–12; puzzles, games, projects; emphasizes geometry.

☆ Cameron, A. J. *Mathematical Enterprises for Schools.* Pergamon, 1966, 188 pp.
>Excellent source for enrichment purposes.

Cathcart, George, ed. *The Mathematics Laboratory: Readings from the "Arithmetic Teacher."* NCTM, 1977, 232 pp.
>Comprehensive treatment: What? Why? When? How?

☆ Charosh, Mannis, ed. *Mathematical Challenges: Selected Problems from the "Mathematics Student Journal."* NCTM, 1965, 135 pp., paper.
>A collection of problems for students in grades 7–12.

☆ Dalton, LeRoy C., and Henry D. Snyder, eds. *Topics for Mathematics Clubs.* NCTM, 1973, 106 pp.

Dumas, Enoch, and C. W. Schminke. *Math Activities for Child Involvement.* 2d ed. Allyn, 1977, 360 pp., paper.

Greenes, Carole E., et al. *Problem Solving in the Mathematics Laboratory: How to Do It.* Prindle, 1972, 166 pp., paper.

Gruenberger, Joyce. *Math Chalk Talk.* Zavell, 1974, 54 pp.

Higgins, Jon L., and Larry A. Sachs. *Mathematics Laboratories: 150 Activities and Games for Elementary Schools.* NCTM, 1974, 230 pp.

Hill, Thomas, ed. *Mathematical Challenges II—plus Six.* NCTM, 1974, 128 pp.

Humphrey, James H., and Dorothy D. Sullivan. *Teaching Slow Learners through Active Games.* Thomas, 1970, 184 pp.
> Consists of three chapters respectively devoted to reading, science, and mathematics; describes over 100 games, emphasizing both the concepts and their applications.

Hurwitz, Abraham B., Arthur Goddard, and David T. Epstein. *More Number Games.* Funk, 1977, 294 pp.
> A companion volume to *Number Games to Improve Your Child's Arithmetic.*

Hynes, Michael C., and Douglas K. Brumbaugh. *Mathematics Activities Handbook for Grades 5–12.* Parker, 1976, 260 pp.

☆ Johnson, Donovan A. *Excursions in Outdoor Measurement.* Walch, 1974, 121 pp., paper.
> A variety of techniques: shadow reckoning, contour mapping, hypsometer, scale drawing, plane table, transit, planimeter, pantograph, spherometer, sundial, and so on.

☆ _____. *Games for Learning Mathematics.* Walch, 1963, 176 pp.
> A description of seventy games involving arithmetic, algebra, and geometry.

☆ Kastner, Bernice. *Applications of Secondary School Mathematics.* NCTM, 1978, 106 pp.
> Realistic applications from physics, chemistry, biology, economics, and music.

☆ Kidd, Kenneth P., Shirley S. Myers, and David M. Cilley. *The Laboratory Approach to Mathematics.* SRA, 1970, 281 pp.

King, Franklin K., and Forest King. *Learning and Teaching the Metric System.* Allyn, 1979, 184 pp., paper.

☆ Krulik, Stephen. *A Handbook of Aids for Teaching Junior-Senior High School Mathematics.* Saunders, 1971, 120 pp.
> A collection of useful games and devices, including tangrams, curve stitching, Tower of Hanoi, and the number-base calendar, among others.

_____. *A Mathematics Laboratory Handbook for Secondary Schools.* Saunders, 1972, 107 pp., paper.

Kulm, Gerald. *Laboratory Activities for Teachers of Secondary Mathematics.* Prindle, 1976, 124 pp.
> Interesting activities, including sphere stacking, balancing points, figurate numbers, radioactive decay, and others; bibliography.

Laycock, Mary, and Connie Johnson. *The Tapestry of Mathematics, a Resource Book for Secondary School Mathematics.* Activity, 1978, 266 pp.

Laycock, Mary, and Gene Watson. *The Fabric of Mathematics: A Resource Book for Teachers.* Activity, 1975, 288 pp.

Maletsky, Evan M., and Christian R. Hirsch, eds. *Activities from the "Mathematics Teacher."* NCTM, 1981, 140 pp.
: Activities that deal with computational skills, calculators, geometry, measurement, and problem solving.

Miller, William A. *Mathematical Puzzles and Games for the Classroom and Resource Center.* Vol. I, *Tic-Tac-Toe and Its Extensions.* Endeavors, 1978, 97 pp., paper.

Mu Alpha Theta. *Mathematical Buds.* NCTM, 1978, 126 pp.
: A collection of eight excellent math-fair essays by secondary and two-year-college students.

☆ National Council of Teachers of Mathematics. *Applications in School Mathematics.* 1979 Yearbook. NCTM, 247 pp.
: Valuable bibliography.

☆ ———. *Enrichment Mathematics for the Grades.* Twenty-seventh Yearbook. NCTM, 1963, 368 pp.
: Bibliographies: "Mathematics for the Gifted," pp. 6-14; "A Graded List of Readers," pp. 195-204; "Mathematics Booklist for School Libraries," pp. 331-40.

☆ ———. *Enrichment Mathematics for High School.* Twenty-eighth Yearbook. NCTM, 1963, 388 pp.
: Bibliographies: "Mathematics for the Gifted," pp. 6-16; "Mathematics Booklist for School Libraries," pp. 379-88.

☆ ———. *Instructional Aids in Mathematics.* Thirty-fourth Yearbook. NCTM, 1973, 442 pp.

Ranucci, Ernest R., and Joseph L. Teeters. *Creating Escher-Type Drawings.* Creative Pubs., 1977, 194 pp., softbound.
: Very informative workbook; bibliography, 18 references.

☆ Reys, Robert, and Thomas Post. *The Mathematics Laboratory: Theory to Practice.* Prindle, 1973, 256 pp.

Rice, Jean. *My Friend the Computer.* Denison, 1976, 85 pp.
: Simple introduction; sixth-grade level; accompanying teaching guide and activity book.

Salkind, Charles T., ed. *The Contest Problem Book.* New Mathematical Library, vol. 5. Random, 1961, 154 pp., paper.
: A collection of problems from the annual high school contests of the Mathematical Association of America.

———. *The MAA Problem Book II.* Random, 1966, 112 pp.
: A collection of problems from the annual high school mathematics contests.

Salkind, Charles T., and James M. Earl. *The MAA Problem Book III.* Random, 1973, 186 pp.
: High school contests of the MAA for the period 1966 to 1972.

☆ Schall, William E. *Activity-oriented Mathematics: Readings for Elementary Teachers.* Prindle, 1976, 481 pp.
: Contains considerable material of interest to middle school and secondary school teachers; more than a hundred articles; extensive bibliography.

Shklarksy (or Shkliarskii), D. O., et al. *The USSR Olympiad Problem Book.* Freeman, 1962, 452 pp., paper.

☆ Sobel, Max A., and Evan M. Maletsky. *Teaching Mathematics: A Sourcebook of Aids, Activities, and Strategies.* Prentice, 1975, 240 pp.

Straszewicz, S. *Mathematical Problems and Puzzles from the Polish Mathematical Olympiads.* Pergamon, 1965, 367 pp.

☆ Suydam, Marilyn N., and Jon L. Higgins. *Activity-based Learning in Elementary School Mathematics.* NCTM, 1977, 178 pp.

Vochko, Lee E., ed. *Manipulative Activities and Games in the Mathematics Classroom.* NEA, 1979, 112 pp.
For elementary, middle grades, and secondary school students.

Wenninger, Magnus. *Spherical Models.* Cambridge, 1979, 145 pp., paper.

Yates, Robert C. *The Trisection Problem.* Classics in Mathematics Education series, vol. 3. NCTM, 1971, 68 pp.

Dictionaries and Handbooks

Baker, Cyril C. T. *Dictionary of Mathematics.* Nelson, 1961; Hart, 1966, 352 pp., cloth and paper.
Concise, but fairly comprehensive.

☆ Bendick, Jeanne, and Marcia Levin. *Mathematics Illustrated Dictionary.* McGraw, 1972, 232 pp.
Fact, figures, and people—including the "new math."

Garcia, Mariano. *Mathematics Dictionary: Spanish-English/English-Spanish.* Hobbs, 1965, 78 pp., paper.

Herland, Leo. *Dictionary of Mathematical Sciences.* Vol. 1, *German-English.* 2d rev. ed. Ungar, 1951, 235 pp.

Hyman, Charles J. *German-English Mathematics Dictionary.* Consultants Bureau (div. of Plenum), 1960, 131 pp.

☆ James, Glenn, and Robert C. James, eds. *Mathematics Dictionary.* 2d ed. Van Nostrand, 1959, 546 pp.
Authoritative; multilingual edition (French, German, Russian, Spanish); more than just a word dictionary; could be described as a "correlated condensation of mathematical concepts."

Karush, William. *The Crescent Dictionary of Mathematics.* Macmillan, 1962, 313 pp.

McDowell, C. H. *A Short Dictionary of Mathematics (Arithmetic, Algebra, Plane Trigonometry and Geometry)*. Littlefield, 1964, 103 pp., paper.
> For beginning students.

MacIntyre, Sheila, and Edith Witte. *German-English Mathematical Vocabulary*. 2d ed. Interscience, 1966, 95 pp.

☆ Marks, Robert W. *The New Mathematics Dictionary and Handbook*. Bantam, 1964, 186 pp., paper.
> Includes thumbnail biographical sketches and tables in addition to the dictionary proper.

Merritt, Frederick S. *Mathematics Manual*. McGraw, 1962, 378 pp.
> Methods and principles of various branches of mathematics for reference, review, and problem solving.

Millington, T. A., and W. Millington. *Dictionary of Mathematics*. Cassell, 1966, 259 pp.

☆ Pemberton, John E. *How to Find Out in Mathematics*. Pergamon, 1963, 158 pp., paper; Macmillan, 1964, paper.
> A practical guide to sources of mathematical information, including careers, encyclopedias, dictionaries, periodicals, bibliographies, mathematical tables, and mathematical societies. A unique and extremely useful book; should be in every library.

☆ *Universal Encyclopedia of Mathematics*. Simon, 1964, cloth; New American, 1964, 715 pp., paper.
> More than a mere dictionary; contains numerous formulas, tables, synopses, methods, and illustrative examples with solutions.

☆ Yates, Robert C. *Curves and Their Properties*. Classics in Mathematics Education series, vol. 4. NCTM, 1974, 259 pp.

Publications of the NCTM

Yearbooks

☆ Thirty-second: *A History of Mathematics Education in the United States and Canada*. 1970, 557 pp.
> Reviews issues and forces related to mathematics curricula and instruction in grades K–12 from colonial days to the present time.

☆ 1978: *Developing Computational Skills*. 1978, 256 pp.
> Eighteen authors look at computational skills, giving a fresh view of teaching basic facts, algorithms, and mental arithmetic, along with ideas on teaching learning disabled children and teaching with a calculator.

☆ 1979: *Applications in School Mathematics*. 1979, 248 pp.
> A multitude of practical, timely applications of mathematics in such diverse fields as environment, finance, human traits, music, and statistics; ideas for immediate classroom use at all grade levels; an annotated bibliography.

☆ 1980: *Problem Solving in School Mathematics*. 1980, 241 pp.
> A collection of twenty-two timely, practical essays that implement the current goal of competency in problem solving in mathematical education.

☆ 1981: *Teaching Statistics and Probability*. 1981, 246 pp.
> Classroom ideas for the preschool level on up; graphs, population sampling, generating random digits, games of chance, stem-and-leaf plots, correlation, a computer algorithm, and more.

☆ 1982: *Mathematics for the Middle Grades (5–9)*. 1982, 246 pp.
> Focuses on practical considerations for today's classroom teacher in grades 5–9.

☆ 1983: *The Agenda in Action*. 1983, 245 pp.
> Takes the *Agenda*'s eight recommendations one by one and shows how teachers can implement them in the classroom.

☆ 1984: *Computers in Mathematics Education*. 1984, 244 pp.
> Discusses computing from the standpoints of its challenge, impact, and perspective and as a diagnostic tool. Discusses programming as a means of teaching mathematics.

☆ 1985: *The Secondary School Mathematics Curriculum*. 1985, 250 pp.
> Charts new curricular directions in terms of content, organization, and priorities. Describes promising curricula that have proved worthy of study and emulation.

☆ 1986: *Estimation and Mental Computation*. 1986, 248 pp.
> Gives the *how to* and *why* of teaching estimation and its companion, mental computation, and presents the broader view of both that technological advances demand.

Classics in Mathematical Education

Because they have a timeless quality about them, the NCTM has authentically reprinted the following books in hardback from so that they may once again be available for the study, enrichment, and enjoyment of the mathematics education community.

Vol. 1. *The Pythagorean Proposition*. Elisha S. Loomis. 1968, 306 pp.
> A historical review, presenting 370 demonstrations of the Pythagorean theorem.

Vol. 3. *The Trisection Problem*. Robert C. Yates. 1971, 68 pp.
> A treatise on one of the three famous problems of antiquity; bibliography.

Vol. 4. *Curves and Their Properties*. Robert C. Yates. 1974, 259 pp.
> Originally published in 1952, a teaching supplement on a variety of unusual, fascinating plane curves.

Vol. 5. *A Rhythmic Approach to Mathematics*. Edith L. Somervell. Preface by Mary Everest Boole. 1975, 72 pp.
> First published in 1906, a unique resource on curve stitching—the art of creating an original design from a geometrical framework. Includes the full-color plates that appeared in the original printing.

Vol. 6. *How to Draw a Straight Line*. A. B. Kempe. 1977, 64 pp.
> First published in London in 1877 as an expanded version of a "Lecture on Linkages."

Vol. 7. *Whom the Gods Love: The Story of Evariste Galois*. Leopold Infeld. 1978, 342 pp.
> First published in 1948, a fascinating biography of a brilliant, passionate young nineteenth century mathematician.

Vol. 8. *The Rhind Mathematical Papyrus.* 1979, 160 pp.
> A reprint of the A. B. Chace edition. The papyrus remains our major source of knowledge about early Egyptian mathematics.

Enrichment and Recreation

A Bibliography of Recreational Mathematics. 4 vols. William L. Schaaf. 1970, 148 pp.; 1970, 191 pp.; 1973, 187 pp.; 1978, 178 pp.
> Vols. 1, 2, and 3 list the best of the literature up to 1973. Vol. 4 updates the material, lists more than 2600 references, most published since 1972, and includes a supplementary glossary of over 200 terms not given in vol. 3.

The Contest Problem Book III, compiled by Charles T. Salkind and James M. Earl. MAA, 1973, 186 pp.
> Problems from the Annual High School Mathematics Examination from 1966 to 1972 and their solutions.

The Contest Problem Book IV, compiled by Ralph A. Artino, Anthony M. Gaglione, and Niel Shell. MAA, 1983, 184 pp.
> Problems from the Annual High School Mathematics Examination from 1973 to 1982 and their solutions.

Geometry Problems My Students Have Written. Ruth Carwell Kespohl. 1979, 87 pp.
> Clever illustrations clarify problems and solutions written by high school students.

How to Develop Problem Solving Using a Calculator. Janet Morris. 1981, 42 pp.
> Activities for upper elementary grades through high school; whole numbers, decimals, percents, geometry; perforated.

How to Enrich Geometry Using String Designs. Victoria Pohl. 1986, 68 pp.
> Step-by-step directions, with abundant illustrations, for constructing string designs on polygons and polyhedra. Grades 6–10 and even older. Removable pages can be duplicated. Enrichment for individual students, groups, or the entire class.

International Mathematical Olympiads 1959-1977. Compiled and with solutions by Samuel L. Greitzer. MAA, 1979, 210 pp.
> Problems and their solutions from the first nineteen years of this international competition.

Leonardo's Dessert: No Pi. Herbert Wills III. 1985, 28 pp.
> Geometry-minded students and teachers will be hooked on Leonardo's method of transforming curvilinear regions into rectangles of the same area without using pi. Filled with fascinating illustrations.

Mathematical Buds. Mu Alpha Theta, 1978, 126 pp.
> Papers done by secondary school and two-year-college students.

Mathematical History: Activities, Puzzles, Stories, and Games. Merle Mitchell. 1978, 74 pp.
> Imaginative puzzles and games based on stories of famous mathematicians, numerals of ancient peoples, and even numerology to enliven the study of mathematics in the middle grades; perforated.

Mathematics and Humor. Edited by Aggie Azzolino, Linda Silvey, and Barnabas Hughes. 1978, 48 pp.
> A collection of jokes, riddles, and cartoons to add levity to bulletin boards and test papers and pique the interest of students from junior high school up.

Mathematics and Science: An Adventure in Postage Stamps. William L. Schaaf. 1978, 152 pp.
> The influence of mathematics on technology and thus on civilization as seen through postage stamps. An exciting chronicle of human achievement with broad appeal.

Mathematics Contests: A Handbook for Mathematics Educators. David R. Johnson and James R. Margenau. 1982, 94 pp.
> Lists mathematics contests by geographic region and outlines procedures for including such competitions in your school, identifying distinctions and advantages of each.

Mathematics Projects Handbook. 2d ed. Adrien L. Hess. 1982, 46 pp.
> Useful guide for junior and senior high school teachers and students in choosing and developing projects. Bibliography.

Mathematics through Paper Folding. Alton T. Olson. 1975, 64 pp.
> Offers active experiences in discovering and demonstrating mathematical relationships.

Polyhedron Models for the Classroom. 2d ed. Magnus J. Wenninger. 1975, 80 pp.
> Seven removable pages of designs to be used as templates to make the models shown in the text; directions and historical notes.

Some "Prime" Comparisons. Stephen I. Brown. 1978, 106 pp.
> A mind-expanding journey into number theory for intellectually alive high school students or students in teacher education courses.

A Sourcebook of Applications of School Mathematics. MAA/NCTM, 1980, 361 pp.
> Reasonable, realistic mathematical applications; secondary school level.

Student Merit Awards: High School. Edited by Leroy Sachs. 1984, 137 pp.
> Challenging, motivational projects to stimulate and recognize mathematics achievement. Units require ten to thirty hours of outside research and writing. Includes teacher notes and an official certificate to reproduce and personalize.

Student Merit Awards: Middle School. Edited by Leroy Sachs. 1984, 100 pp.
> Same as high school booklet above, but projects are less difficult.

Topics for Mathematics Clubs. 2d ed. Edited by LeRoy C. Dalton and Henry D. Snyder. 1983, 106 pp.
> Stimulates interest in mathematical investigation through exciting topics not usually discussed in the classroom; bibliographies.

Research

Classroom Ideas from Research on Secondary School Mathematics. Donald Dessart and Marilyn Suydam. 1983, 128 pp.
> Simplifies recent research findings on teaching algebra and geometry. Principal ideas for the classroom are highlighted.

Learning and Mathematics Games. George Bright, John Harvey, and Margariete Wheeler.
> Describes elementary and secondary classroom studies that investigated the use of selected games to promote learning.

Mathematics Teaching Today: Perspectives from Three National Surveys. James T. Fey. 1981, 30 pp.
> Interpretations of the findings of three NSF studies, which included a large-scale survey of teachers and administrators, case studies of individual schools, and a review of the literature.

Research in Mathematics Education. Edited by Richard J. Shumway. 1980, 487 pp.
> A definitive professional reference; discusses the research process in detail; current status of research, trends, issues, and specific promising hypotheses.

Research within Reach: Secondary School Mathematics. Mark Driscoll. Research and Development Interpretation Service. 1983, 179 pp.
> Research chosen in response to questions asked by classroom teachers and then interpreted so it could be of highest benefit to them.

Results from the Second Mathematics Assessment of the National Assessment of Educational Progress. 1981, 167 pp.
> Interprets results and highlights changes since the first assessment.

Soviet Studies in the Psychology of Learning and Teaching Mathematics. 14 vols. Edited by Jeremy Kilpatrick, Izaak Wirszup, Edward Begle, and James Wilson. 1969-75.
  Vol. 1—*The Learning of Mathematical Concepts*) 216 pp.
  Vol. 2—*The Structure of Mathematical Abilities,* 128 pp.
  Vol. 3—*Problem Solving in Arithmetic and Algebra,* 183 pp.
  Vol. 4—*Problem Solving in Geometry,* 154 pp.
  Vol. 5—*The Development of Spatial Abilities,* 168 pp.
  Vol. 6—*Instruction in Problem Solving,* 136 pp.
  Vol. 7—*Children's Capacity for Learning Mathematics,* 261 pp.
  Vol. 8—*Methods of Teaching Mathematics,* 271 pp.
  Vol. 9—*Problem-solving Processes of Mentally Retarded Children,* 170 pp.
  Vol. 10—*Teaching Mathematics to Mentally Retarded Children,* 224 pp.
  Vol. 11—*Analysis and Synthesis as Problem-solving Methods,* 171 pp.
  Vol. 12—*Problems of Instruction,* 172 pp.
  Vol. 13—*Analyses of Reasoning Processes,* 231 pp.
  Vol. 14—*Teaching Arithmetic in the Elementary School,* 202 pp.

General Publications

An Agenda for Action: Recommendations for School Mathematics of the 1980s. 1980, 29 pp.
> Based on information from a series of studies funded by the NSF and from two mathematics assessments of the NAEP; outlines future directions for mathematics education.

Alternative Courses for Secondary School Mathematics. Edited by Marilyn Suydam. 1985, 57 pp.
> Designed to stimulate innovative, exemplary curriculum development, this booklet describes new courses in use in the U. S. and Canada.

Changing School Mathematics: A Responsive Process. Edited by Jack Price and J. D. Gawronski. 1981, 229 pp.
> Discusses the process of change and the strategies for implementing change and then applies this knowledge to changing mathematics programs.

Computing and Mathematics: The Impact on Secondary School Curricula. Edited by James T. Fey and others. 1984, 100 pp.
> Deals in a general way with the effect of computing technology on school mathematics, the propects for change, and its specific impact on such disciplines as algebra, geometry, and calculus.

Dancing Curves: A Dynamic Demonstration of Geometric Principles. Merwin J. Lyng. 1978, 16 pp.
> Instructions for constructing a string model to be used with light beams to dynamically illustrate conic sections as well as lines, curves, and surfaces. Includes four color slides.

Deductive Systems: Finite and Non-Euclidean Geometries. Garth E. Runion and James R. Lockwood. 1978, 90 pp.
> Two non-Euclidean systems are considered as a means of strengthening the student's awareness and understanding of the deductive systems of mathematics in general. For high school and college levels.

Films in the Mathematics Classroom. Barbara Bestgen and Robert Reys. 1982, 90 pp.
> A listing of films with pertinent data and two reviews of each, one by the distributor and one by a classroom teacher. Each film is rated on a scale of 0 to 4.

Guidelines for Evaluating Computerized Instructional Materials. 2d ed. William Heck, Jerry Johnson, Robert J. Kansky, and Dick Dennis. 1984, 32 pp.
> An up-to-date revision of the popular guidelines that have given thousands of teachers and administrators concise, practical help for slicing through the maze of materials in the software jungle.

Guidelines for the Preparation of Teachers of Mathematics. 2d ed. 1981, 29 pp.
> Prepared by NCTM's Commission on the Education of Teachers of Mathematics.

Guidelines for the Tutor of Mathematics. Henry S. Kepner, Jr., and David R. Johnson. 1977, 32 pp.
> Ideas and encouragement for the high school student tutor who, although successful in mathematics, may lack teaching skills.

HM Math Study Skills Program. Catherine D. Tobin. NCTM/NASSP. 1980; Teacher's Guide, 60 pp.; Student Text, 95 pp.
> A prealgebra program for reinforcing study skills in problem solving, study habits, estimating, test taking, and so on.

How to Evaluate Mathematics Textbooks. Based on the guide published by the Virginia Council of Teachers of Mathematics. 1982, 8 pp.
> This concise aid discusses evaluative criteria and contains a simple rating system that makes the subjective task of evaluation more objective.

How to Evaluate Your Mathematics Program. 1981, 18 pp.
> A tool for assessing program effectiveness and setting directions for change. Developed by teachers, principals, and supervisors from elementary, secondary, and higher education.

How to Study Mathematics. James Margenau and Michael Sentlowitz. 1977, 32 pp.
> A readable, appealing self-help for the struggling but earnest junior or senior high school student; contains captivating cartoons and a list of diagnoses and prescriptions.

The Mathematical Education of Exceptional Children and Youth: An Interdisciplinary Approach. Edited by Vincent J. Glennon. 1981, 408 pp.
> An exhaustive professional reference; each essay is directed to a particular exceptionality—visually handicapped, learning disabled, the gifted, and so on.

Mathematics Tests Available in the United States and Canada. 5th ed. Compiled by James S. Braswell and Douglas T. Owens. 1981, 32 pp.
> Enlarged and updated; lists tests by author, grade levels and forms, availability of norms, publisher, and reference in *Mental Measurements Yearbook*.

Practical Ways to Teach the Basic Mathematical Skills. VCTM (Virginia Council of Teachers of Mathematics). 1979, 202 pp.
> Addresses the ten basic skills, as defined by the National Council of Supervisors of Mathematics.

Priorities in School Mathematics: An Executive Summary. 1981, 33 pp.
> Reports findings of the NSF-funded PRISM project; abundant graphs.

Problem Solving in the Mathematics Classroom. Edited by Sid Rachlin. Mathematics Council of the Alberta Teachers' Association. 1984, 175 pp.
> Essays from teachers in the U.S. and Canada organized into four parts: Understanding the Problem, Devising a Plan, Carrying Out the Plan, and Looking Back–Looking Ahead. Includes exercises and teaching strategies.

Professional Development for Teachers of Mathematics: A Handbook. Author team headed by Ross Taylor. 1986, 66 pp.
> Offers an overview of the issues of professional development, gives guidelines for arranging effective PD activities, and suggests ways of finding resources for such activities.

Readings in the History of Mathematics Education. Edited by James K. Bidwell and Robert G. Clason. 1970, 706 pp.
> Source materials complementary to the Thirty-second Yearbook. Contains committee reports and other primary source documents commonly cited but not readily available.

Resources for Teaching Mathematics in Bilingual Classrooms. C. James Lovett and Ted Snyder. ERIC. 1980, 56 pp.
> Overview of issues and problems; annotated bibliography of materials for Spanish/English programs.

So You're a Mathematics Supervisor. Ross Taylor. 1981, 20 pp.
> Practical ideas to help new mathematics supervisors to relate effectively with others, develop leadership in teachers, enhance their personal leadership qualities, and use their time efficiently.

Was Pythagoras Chinese? Frank J. Swetz and T. I. Kao. NCTM/Pennsylvania State University Press. 1977, 75 pp.
> An examination of right triangle theory in ancient China.

Readings from NCTM Periodicals

Activities for Implementing Curricular Themes from the Agenda for Action. Edited by Christian R. Hirsch. 1986, 204 pp.
> Activities selected from recent issues of the *Mathematics Teacher* to reinforce the NCTM's recommendations for school mathematics of the 1980s. Focus is on problem solving, basic skills, calculators, computers, and manipulatives.

Activities for Junior High School and Middle School Mathematics: Readings from the "Arithmetic Teacher" and the "Mathematics Teacher." Compiled by Kenneth E. Easterday, Loren L. Henry, and F. Morgan Simpson. 1981, 218 pp.
> Selected activities conveniently organized by strands, including counting and place value; decimals, fractions, and percents; probability and statistics; and problem solving.

Activities from the "Mathematics Teacher." Edited by Evan M. Maletsky and Christian R. Hirsch. 1981, 140 pp.
> Useful source of discovery lessons, laboratory experiences, mathematical games and puzzles, and model constructions for grades 7-12; perforated.

IDEAS from the Arithmetic Teacher: Grades 6–8 Middle School. George Immerzeel and Melvin Thomas. 1982, 142 pp.
> Activities are grouped by the topics of computation, fractions and decimals, number patterns, flowcharts, problem solving, geometry, and metric measure. Tear-out pages for easy duplication.

"Gifted Students." (*MT*, April 1983, 90 pp.)
> Articles characterizing the special needs of the mathematically gifted and presenting alternative programs and curricula to meet their needs.

"Geometry." (*MT*, September, 1985, 90 pp.)
> Ideas on teaching geometry: some new insights and some departures from tradition, including genuinely new options with computerized microworlds.

"Minorities and Mathematics." (*JRME*, March 1984, 93 pp.)
> A compilation of papers that examine and attempt to synthesize the research on minorities and mathematics in the U.S. today.

Publications of the Mathematical Association of America

The New Mathematical Library
1. *Numbers: Rational and Irrational.* Ivan Niven. 1961, 136 pp.
2. *What Is Calculus About?* W. W. Sawyer. 1961, 118 pp.
3. *An Introduction to Inequalities.* E. F. Beckenbach and R. Bellman. 1961, 133 pp.
4. *Geometric Inequalities.* N. D. Kazarinoff. 1961, 132 pp.
5. *Contest Problem Book I.* Charles T. Salkind. 1961, 154 pp.
6. *The Lore of Large Numbers.* P. J. Davis. 1961, 165 pp.
7. *Uses of Infinity.* Leo Zippin. 1962, 151 pp.
8. *Geometric Transformations.* I. M. Yaglom. 1962, 133 pp.
9. *Continued Fractions.* Carl D. Olds. 1963, 162 pp.
10. *Graphs and Their Uses.* Oystein Ore. 1963, 131 pp.
11. *Hungarian Problem Book I.* (Eötvös Competitions, 1894-1905). 1963, 111 pp.

12. *Hungarian Problem Book II.* (Eötvös Competitions, 1906-1928). 1963, 120 pp.
13. *Episodes from the Early History of Mathematics.* Asger Aaboe. 1964, 133 pp.
14. *Groups and Their Graphs.* I. Grossman and W. Magnus. 1964, 195 pp.
15. *The Mathematics of Choice.* Ivan Niven. 1965, 202 pp.
16. *From Pythagoras to Einstein.* K. O. Friedrichs. 1965, 88 pp.
17. *Contest Problem Book II.* C. T. Salkind. 1966, 112 pp.
18. *First Concepts of Topology.* W. G. Chinn and N. E. Steenrod. 1966, 161 pp.
19. *Geometry Revisited.* H. S. M. Coxeter and S. L. Greitzer. 1967, 193 pp.
20. *Invitation to Number Theory.* Oystein Ore. 1967, 129 pp.
21. *Geometric Transformations II.* I. M. Yaglom. 1968, 189 pp.
22. *Elementary Cryptanalysis.* Abraham Sinkov. 1966, 189 pp.
23. *Ingenuity in Mathematics.* Ross Honsberger. 1970, 204 pp.
24. *Geometric Transformations III.* I. M. Yaglom. Translated by Abe Shenitzer. 1973, 237 pp.
25. *Contest Problem Book III.* C. T. Salkind and J. M. Earl. 1973, 186 pp.
26. *Mathematical Methods in Science.* George Polya. 1977, 234 pp.
27. *International Mathematical Olympiads—1959-1977.* S. L. Greitzer. 1978, 210 pp.
28. *The Mathematics of Games and Gambling.* Edward W. Packel. 1981, 151 pp.
29. *The Contest Problem Book IV.* R. A. Artino, A. M. Gaglione, and Niel Shell. 1983, 184 pp.
30. *The Role of Mathematics in Science.* Leon Bowden and M. M. Schiffer. 1984, 220 pp.

Periodicals and Journals

Note: Subscription rates quoted below are subject to change.

American Mathematical Monthly. (10 issues a year; membership subscription $48.) Mathematical Association of America, 1529 Eighteenth St., N.W., Washington, DC 20036.

Arithmetic Teacher. (9 a year; membership subscription $35; institutional $40.) Managing Editor, Harry B. Tunis. National Council of Teachers of Mathematics, 1906 Association Dr., Reston, VA 22091.

Australian Mathematics Teacher. (4 a year; $20 Australian.) Business Manager, AMT, 20 Kookaburra St., Kenmore Hills, Queensland, Australia 4069.

The College Mathematics Journal. (5 a year; $39.) Mathematical Association of America, 1529 Eighteenth St., N.W., Washington, DC 20036.

Creative Computing. (6 a year; $8; institutional $15.) Creative Computing, P.O. Box 789-M, Morristown, NJ 07960.

Crux Mathematicorum. (Monthly except July/Aug.; $25 Canadian.) Managing Editor, Kenneth S. Williams, Canadian Mathematical Society, 577 King Edward Ave., Ottawa, ON, Canada K1N 6N5.

Educational Studies in Mathematics. (4 a year; $32; institutional $80.) Editor, Alan J. Bishop, University of Cambridge, United Kingdom. D. Reidel Publishing Co., 190 Old Derby St., Hingham, MA 02043. Back issues, vols. 1-16, $32 a volume; institutional $70.

Eureka, The Archimedeans' Journal. (1 a year.) For subscription rates, write to Business Manager, *Eureka,* The Arts School, Benet St., Cambridge, England.

Fibonacci Quarterly. (4 a year; $25.) Editor, G. E. Bergum. Mathematics Department, Santa Clara University, Santa Clara, CA 95053.

Investigations in Mathematics Education: Expanded Abstracts and Critical Analyses of Recent Research. ($8.00 a year, $2.75 a single copy; $1.00 additional for Canada, $3.00 additional for foreign mailings.) Marilyn N. Suydam, ERIC Clearinghouse for Science, Mathematics, and Environmental Education, 1200 Chambers Rd., Columbus, OH 43212.

Journal for Research in Mathematics Education. (5 a year; NCTM members, $12; others, $15.) Editor, Jeremy Kilpatrick. National Council of Teachers of Mathematics, 1906 Association Dr., Reston, VA 22091.

Journal of Recreational Mathematics. (4 a year; individuals $12.50; institutions $40.00; postage $3.00 U.S. and Canada; $7.00 elsewhere.) Joseph Madachy, Editor, Baywood Publishing Co., 120 Marine St., Farmingdale, NY 11735.

Mathematical Gazette. (4 a year; £8.50.) The Mathematical Association, 259 London Rd., Leicester LE2 3BE, England.

Mathematical Log. (4 a year; $2.00 US, $3.50 foreign.) Journal of Mu Alpha Theta (national high school and junior college mathematics clubs), 601 Elm Ave., Room 423, Norman, OK 73019.

Mathematics in School. (5 a year; £8.50.) The Mathematical Association, 259 London Rd., Leicester LE2 3BE, England.

Mathematics Magazine. (5 a year; $36.) Mathematical Association of America, 1529 Eighteenth St., N.W., Washington, DC 20036.

Mathematics Teacher. (9 a year; membership subscription $35; institutional $40.) Managing Editor, Harry B. Tunis. National Council of Teachers of Mathematics, 1906 Association Dr., Reston, VA 22091.

Mathematics Teaching. (4 a year; £14 by standing order.) Association of Teachers of Mathematics, Kings Chambers, Queen St., Derby DE1 3DA, England.

The Pentagon. (2 a year; $5 for two years.) Dept. of Mathematics, Western Illinois University, Macomb, IL 61455.

Pi Mu Epsilon Journal. (2 a year; $4 for two years; nonmembers $6 for two years.) Joe Konhauser, Editor, Math Department, Macalester College, Saint Paul, MN 55105.

School Science and Mathematics. (8 a year; membership subscription $11; institutional $14.) School Science and Mathematics Association, P.O. Box 1614, Indiana, PA 15705.

Scientific American. (12 a year; $18.) 415 Madison Ave., New York, NY 10017.

The Two-Year College Mathematics Journal. (See *The College Mathematics Journal.*)

University of Oklahoma News Letter. (4 a year.) University of Oklahoma, Norman, OK 73069.

Appendix: Directory of Current Publishers

Abbeville. Abbeville Press, 505 Park Ave., New York, NY 10022.
Ablex. Ablex Publishing Corp., 355 Chestnut St., Norwood, NJ 07648.
Abt. Abt Books, 55 Wheeler St., Cambridge, MA 02138.
Academic. Academic Press, 111 Fifth Ave., New York, NY 10003
Activity. Activity Resources Co., P.O. Box 4875, Hayward, CA 94540.
Addison. Addison-Wesley Publishing Co., 508 South St., Reading, MA 01867.
Allen. Allen & Unwin, 9 Winchester Terr., Winchester, MA 01890.
Allyn. Allyn & Bacon, 7 Wells Ave., Newton, MA 02159.
Appleton. Appleton-Century-Crofts, 25 Van Zant St., East Norwalk, CT 06855.
Arco. Arco Publications, 29 Great Portland St., London, W.1, England.
Atheneum. Atheneum Publishers, 597 Fifth Ave., New York, NY 10017.
Avon. Avon Books, 1790 Broadway, New York, NY 10019.
B. and N. Barnes & Noble, 10 E. 53d St., New York, NY 10022.
Bailey. Bailey Brothers & Swinfen, Warner House, Wear Bay Rd., Bowles Well Gardens, Folkestone, Kent, England.
Bantam. Bantam Books, 666 Fifth Ave., New York, NY 10103.
Barnes. A. S. Barnes & Co., 9601 Aero Dr., San Diego, CA 92123.
Basic. Basic Books, 10 E. 53d St., New York, NY 10022.
Benjamin. Benjamin-Cummings Publishing Co., 2727 Sand Hill Rd., Menlo Park, CA 94025.
Berks. Berks Solar Center, Box 385, R.D. #4, Boyertown, PA 19512.
Birkhäuser. Birkhäuser Boston, 380 Green St., Cambridge, MA 02139.
Blackie. Blackie & Son, Glasgow. Order from Interscience, unless otherwise stated.
Book-Lab. Book-Lab, 500 74th St., North Bergen, NJ 07047.
Boyd. Boyd and Fraser Publishing Co., 3627 Sacramento St., San Francisco, CA 94118.
Brooks. Brooks/Cole Publishing Co., 555 Abrego, Monterey, CA 93940.
Brown. William C. Brown Group, 2460 Kerper Blvd., Dubuque, IA 52001.
Burgundy. Burgundy Press, P.O. Box 313, Southampton, PA 18966.
Cambridge. Cambridge University Press, 32 E. 57th St., New York, NY 10022.
Camelot. Camelot Publishing Co., P.O. Box 1357, Ormond Beach, FL 32074.
Canfield. Canfield Press, San Francisco. Order from Harper & Row, Scranton, PA 18512.
Cassell. Cassell & Co., 35 Red Lion Sq., London, W.C. 1, England.
Chelsea. Chelsea Publishing Co., 432 Park Ave. S., New York, NY 10016.
Chicago. University of Chicago Press, 5801 Ellis Ave., Chicago, IL 60637.
Citadel. Citadel Press, 120 Enterprise Ave., Secaucus, NJ 07094.
Clearvue. Clearvue, Inc., 5711 N. Milwaukee Ave., Chicago, IL 60646.
Clearinghouse. International Clearinghouse, Science Teaching Center, University of Maryland, College Park, MD 20742.
Collier. Collier Books, 866 Third Ave., New York, NY 10022.
Columbia. Columbia University Press, 562 W. 113th St., New York, NY 10025.
Computer. Computer Science Press, 11 Taft Ct., Rockville, MD 20850.
Cornerstone. Cornerstone Library, 1230 Avenue of the Americas, New York, NY 10020.

Creative. Creative Computing Press, One Park Ave., New York, NY 10016.
Creative Pubs. Creative Publications, 1101 San Antonio Rd., Suite 101, Mountain View, CA 94043.
Creative Tchg. Creative Teaching Associates, P.O. Box 7714, Fresno, CA 93727.
Crowell. Crowell Collier & Macmillan, 866 Third Ave., New York, NY 10022.
Cuisenaire. Cuisenaire Company of America, 12 Church St., Box D, New Rochelle, NY 10802.
Cummings. Benjamin-Cummings Publishing Co., 2727 Sand Hill Rd., Menlo Park, CA 94025.
Dekker. Marcel Dekker, 270 Madison Ave., New York, NY 10016.
Dell. Dell Publishing Co., One Dag Hammarskjold Plaza, New York, NY 10017.
Denison. T. S. Denison & Co., 9601 Newton Ave., Minneapolis, MN 55437.
Dial. Dial Press, c/o Doubleday & Co., 501 Franklin Ave., Garden City, NY 11530.
Digital. Digital Press, 30 North Ave., Burlington, MA 01803.
Dodd. Dodd, Mead & Co., 79 Madison Ave., New York, NY 10016.
Doubleday. Doubleday & Co., 245 Park Ave., New York, NY 10167.
Dover. Dover Publications, 31 E. Second St., Mineola, NY 11501.
Duell. Duell, Sloane & Pearce. Order from Meredith.
Dutton. E. P. Dutton, 2 Park Ave., New York, NY 10016.
Emerson. Emerson Books, Madelyn Ave., Verplanck, NY 10596.
Endeavors. Creative Endeavors, 407 E. Grand Ave., Mt. Pleasant, MI 48858.
English. English Universities Press. Order from Macmillan.
ERA. ERA Press, Education Research Associates, Box 767, Amherst, MA 01004.
ERIC. ERIC Clearinghouse for Science, Mathematics and Environmental Education, 1200 Chambers Rd., Room 310, Columbus, OH 43212.
Faber. Faber & Faber, 3 Queen Sq., London WC1N 3 AU, Great Britain.
Farrar. Farrar, Straus & Giroux, 19 Union Sq. West, New York, NY 10003.
FCTM. Florida Council of Teachers of Mathematics, College of Education, University of South Florida, Tampa, FL 33620.
Franklin. The Franklin Institute Press, Box 2266, Philadelphia, PA 19103.
Free. The Free Press, 866 Third Ave., New York, NY 10022.
Freeman. W. H. Freeman & Co., 660 Market St., San Francisco, CA 94104.
Funk. Funk & Wagnalls, 53 E. 77 St., New York, NY 10021.
Ginn. Ginn-Blaisdell. Write Ginn & Co., 191 Spring St., Lexington, MA 02173.
Glencoe. Glencoe Press, 17337 Ventura Blvd., Encino, CA 91316.
Graylock. Graylock Press, 428 E. Preston St., Baltimore, MD 21202.
Greenwood. Greenwood Press, Box 5007, 88 Post Rd. W., Westport, CT 06881.
Grosset. Grosset & Dunlap, 51 Madison Ave., New York, NY 10010.
Hafner. Hafner Publishing Co., 866 Third Ave., New York, NY 10022.
Halsted. Halsted Press, 605 Third Ave., New York, NY 10158.
Harcourt. Harcourt Brace Jovanovich. 757 Third Ave., New York, NY 10017.
Harper. Harper & Row, Publishers, 10 E. 53d St., New York, NY 10022.
Hart. Hart Publishing Co., 24 Fifth Ave., New York, NY 10011.
Harvard. Harvard University Press, 79 Garden St., Cambridge, MA 02138.
Hayden. Hayden Book Co., Educational, 10 Mulholland Dr., Hasbrouck Heights, NJ 07604.
Heath. D. C. Heath & Co., 125 Spring St., Lexington, MA 02173.
Heinemann. Heinemann Educational Books, 4 Front St., Exeter, NH 03833.
Hill. Hill & Wang. Order from Farrar.
Holden. Holden-Day, 4432 Telegraph Ave., Oakland, CA 94609.

Holiday. Holiday House, 18 E. 53d St., New York, NY 10022.
Holt. Holt, Rinehart & Winston, 521 Fifth Ave., New York, NY 10175.
Hopkins. Johns Hopkins University Press, Baltimore, MD 21218.
Houghton. Houghton Mifflin Co., One Beacon St., Boston, MA 02107.
Humanities. Humanities Press, 171 First Ave., Atlantic Highlands, NJ 07716.
I.B.M. I.B.M. Direct, Dept. TT4, 1 Culver Rd., Dayton, NJ 08810.
Import. Order from Imported Publications, 320 West Ohio St., Chicago, IL 60610-4175.
Indiana. Indiana University Press, Tenth and Morton Sts., Bloomington, IN 47405.
International. International Council for Computers in Education, University of Oregon, 1787 Agate St., Eugene, OR 97403-1923.
Interscience. c/o John Wiley & Sons, Interscience Division, 605 Third Ave., New York, NY 10158.
Jossey. Jossey-Bass, Publishers, 433 California St., San Francisco, CA 94104.
Kaufmann. William Kaufmann, 95 First St., Los Altos, CA 94022.
Knopf. Alfred A. Knopf, 201 E. 50th St., New York, NY 10022.
Krieger. R. E. Krieger Publishing Co., Box 542, Huntington, NY 11743.
Lewis. A. F. Lewis & Co., 79 Madison Ave., New York, NY 10016.
Lippincott. J. B. Lippincott Co., E. Washington Sq., Philadelphia, PA 19105.
Little. Little, Brown & Co., 34 Beacon St., Boston, MA 02106.
Littlefield. Littlefield, Adams & Co., 81 Adams Dr., Totowa, NJ 07512.
London. University of London Press. Order from British Book Centre, 40 W. 67th St., New York, NY 10019.
Longmans. Longmans Green & Co. Order from David McKay Co., 2 Park Ave., New York, NY 10016.
MAA. Mathematical Association of America, 1529 Eighteenth St., N.W., Washington, DC 20036.
McGraw. McGraw-Hill Book Co., 1221 Avenue of the Americas, New York, NY 10020.
Macmillan. Macmillan Publishing Co., 866 Third Ave., New York, NY 10022.
Mentor. Mentor Books. Order from New American.
Meredith. Meredith Corp., 1716 Locust St., Des Moines, IA 50336.
Merrill. Charles E. Merrill Publishing Co., 936 Eastwind Dr., Westerville, OH 43081.
Messner. Julian Messner, 1230 Avenue of the Americas, New York, NY 10020.
Methuen. Methuen & Co., 733 Third Ave., New York, NY 10017.
MIT. M.I.T. Press, 28 Carleton St., Cambridge, MA 02142.
Moore. Moore Publishing Co., 136 S. Wesler Ave., Oak Park, IL 60302.
Morrow. William Morrow & Co., 105 Madison Ave., New York, NY 10016.
Mu Alpha Theta. Mu Alpha Theta, The University of Oklahoma, Norman, OK 73069.
Murray. John Murray, 65 Clerkenwell Rd., London, EC1R 5BQ England.
N. Carolina. University of North Carolina Press, P.O. Box 2288, Chapel Hill, NC 27514.
NCTM. National Council of Teachers of Mathematics, 1906 Association Dr., Reston, VA 22091.
NEA. National Education Association, Order Department, Box 509, West Haven, CT 06516.
Nelson. Thomas Nelson, Nelson Place at Elm Hill Pike, Nashville, TN 37203.
New American. New American Library, 1633 Broadway, New York, NY 10019.
Norton. W. W. Norton & Co., 500 Fifth Ave., New York, NY 10110.
NYU. New York University Press, Washington Sq., New York, NY 10003.
Ohio. Ohio University Press, Scott Quadrangle, Room 144, Athens, OH 45701.
Oldbourne. Oldbourne Book Co., 1-5 Portpool La., Gray's Inn Rd., London, E.C.1, England.
Open. Open Court Publishing Co., Box 599, 1058 Eighth St., La Salle, IL 61301.

Oryx. Oryx Press, 2214 N. Central Ave., Phoenix, AZ 85004-1483.
Oxford. Oxford University Press, 200 Madison Ave., New York, NY 10016.
Paddington. Order from Grosset.
Parker. Parker Publishing Co., 1 Village Sq., West Nyack, NY 10994.
Pelican. Pelican Books. Order from Penguin.
Penguin. Penguin Books. 40 W. 23d St., New York, NY 10010.
Pergamon. Pergamon Press, Maxwell House, Fairview Park, Elmsford, NY 10523.
Phillips. S. G. Phillips, P.O. Box 83, Chatham, NY 12037.
Philosophical. Philosophical Library, 200 W. 57th St., New York, NY 10019.
Pitman. Pitman Publishing, 1020 Plain St., Marshfield, MA 02050.
Plenum. Plenum Publishing Corp., 233 Spring St., New York, NY 10013.
Potter. Clarkson N. Potter (Crown Publishers), One Park Ave., New York, NY 10016.
Praeger. Praeger Publishers, 521 Fifth Ave., New York, NY 10175.
Prentice. Prentice-Hall, Englewood Cliffs, NJ 07632.
Primary. Primary Press, Box 105a, Parker Ford, PA 19457.
Princeton. Princeton University Press, Princeton, NJ 08540.
Prindle. Prindle, Weber & Schmidt, 20 Park Plaza, Boston, MA 02116-4501.
Putnam. The Putnam Publishing Group, 200 Madison Ave., New York, NY 10016.
Ram. Atma Ram & Sons, Booksellers & Publishers, 1376, Kashmere Gate, Delhi-110006, India.
Random. Random House, 201 E. 50th St., New York, NY 10022.
Reidel. D. Reidel Publishing Co., 190 Old Derby St., Hingham, MA 02043.
Rensselaer. Rensselaer Polytechnic Institute, Troy, NY 12181.
Saunders. Saunders College Publishing, 383 Madison Ave., New York, NY 10017.
Schocken. Schocken Books, 200 Madison Ave., New York, NY 10016.
Science. Science Research Associates, 155 N. Wacker Dr., Chicago, IL 60606.
Scott. Scott, Foresman & Co., 1900 E. Lake Ave., Glenview, IL 60025.
Scribner. Charles Scribner's Sons, 597 Fifth Ave., New York, NY 10017.
Silver. Silver Burdett Co., 250 James St., Morristown, NJ 07960.
Simon. Simon & Schuster, 1230 Avenue of the Americas, New York, NY 10020.
Singer. Random House/Singer School Div., 201 E. 50th St., New York, NY 10022.
SMEAC. Science, Mathematics, and Environmental Education, Information Reference Center, Room 310, 1200 Chambers Rd., Columbus, OH 43212.
Smith. Peter Smith, 6 Lexington Ave., Magnolia, MA 01930.
Spartan. Spartan Books, 432 Park Ave. S., New York, NY 10016.
Springer. Springer-Verlag New York, 175 Fifth Ave., New York, NY 10010.
SRA. Science Research Associates, 155 N. Wacker Dr., Chicago, IL 60606.
Stein. Stein & Day Publishers, Scarborough House, Briarcliff Manor, NY 10510.
Sterling. Sterling Publishing Co., 2 Park Ave., New York, NY 10016.
Sterling Swift. Sterling Swift Publishing Co., 7901 S. IH-35, Austin, TX 78744.
St. Martin's. St. Martin's Press, 175 Fifth Ave., New York, NY 10010.
Taylor. Taylor & Francis, 242 Cherry St., Philadelphia, PA 19106-1906.
Teachers. Teachers College Press, Teachers College, Columbia University, 1234 Amsterdam Ave., New York, NY 10027.
Thames. Thames & Hudson, 500 Fifth Ave., New York, NY 10010.
Thomas. Charles C. Thomas, Publisher, 2600 S. First St., Springfield, IL 62717.
Toronto. University of Toronto Press, St. George Campus, Toronto, ON M5S 1A6, Canada.

Transworld. Transworld Publishers, Cavendish House, 57-59 Uxbridge Rd., Ealing, London W5 5SA, England.

Tuttle. Charles E. Tuttle Co., Tokyo, Japan, and 28 S. Main St., Rutland, VT 05701.

UNESCO. United Nations Sales Section, Publishing Service, New York, NY 10017.

Ungar. Frederick Ungar Publishing Co., 250 Park Ave. S., New York, NY 10003.

Unipub. Unipub, 205 E. 42d St., New York, NY 10017.

University. University Press of America, 4720 Boston Way, Lanham, MD 20801.

U.S.G.P.O. Superintendent of Documents, Government Printing Office, Washington, DC 20402.

Van Nostrand. Van Nostrand Reinhold Co., 135 W. 50th St., New York, NY 10020.

Vantage. Vantage Press, 516 W. 34th St., New York, NY 10001.

Viking. Viking Press, 40 W. 23d St., New York, NY 10010.

Vintage. Vintage Books. 201 E. 50th St., New York, NY 10022.

Wadsworth. Wadsworth Publishing Co., 10 Davis Dr., Belmont, CA 94002.

Walch. J. Weston Walch, Box 658, 321 Valley St., Portland, ME 04104.

Walker. Walker & Co., 720 Fifth Ave., New York, NY 10019.

Watts. Franklin Watts, 387 Park Ave. S., New York, NY 10016.

Webster. Webster Division, McGraw-Hill Book Co., 1221 Avenue of the Americas, New York, NY 10020.

West. West Publishing Co., 50 W. Kellogg Blvd., P.O. Box 43526, Saint Paul, MN 55165.

Westminster. Westminster Press, 925 Chestnut St., Philadelphia, PA 19107.

Wiley. John Wiley & Sons, 605 Third Ave., New York, NY 10158.

Williams. Williams & Wilkins Co., 428 E. Preston St., Baltimore, MD 21202.

Wisconsin. Wisconsin Research and Development Center for Individualized Schooling, Center Document Service, 1025 W. Johnson St., Madison, WI 53706.

World. World University Library, McGraw-Hill Book Co., 1221 Avenue of the Americas, New York, NY 10020.

Worth. Worth Publishers, 444 Park Ave. S., New York, NY 10016.

Yale. Yale University Press, 302 Temple St., New Haven, CT 06520.